Fee-Based

Information Services

Fee-Based Information Services

A Study of a Growing Industry

Lorig Maranjian
and
Richard W. Boss

INFORMATION MANAGEMENT SERIES/1

R. R. Bowker Company
New York & London, 1980

Z
674
.5
.U5M37

Published by R. R. Bowker Company
1180 Avenue of the Americas, New York, N.Y. 10036
Copyright © 1980 by Xerox Corporation
All rights reserved
Printed and bound in the United States of America

Library of Congress Cataloging in Publication Data

Maranjian, Lorig.
  Fee-based information services.

  (Information management series)
  Bibliography: p.
  Includes index.
  1. Information services—United States. I. Boss,
Richard W., joint author. II. Title. III. Series.
Z674.5.U5M37   025.5'23   80-20176
ISBN 0-8352-1287-4

CONTENTS

PREFACE

This is the first major study in the United States of fee-based information services, a sector of the information industry. The authors have developed a profile of the commercial firms and free-lancers that gather data and undertake limited analysis for a fee, using the methods of traditional librarianship supplemented with on-line literature searching, telephone interviewing, field staff, and a variety of other techniques.

During the early to mid-1970s, the terms "information brokering" and "information brokerage" were commonly used to describe these services, even though many in the field disliked such titles because they evoked images of real estate and commodities firms. Several small companies and free-lancers continue to identify themselves as "information brokers," but others now use "information specialist," "information consultant," "information retailer," or "information service."

When interviewed as part of the research survey for this book, principals in the larger firms indicated a marked preference for "information service" and "fee-based information service." These titles now appear to be in common use both in the United States and abroad. The authors have, therefore, chosen to use "fee-based information services" as the title.

Change is the word to characterize fee-based information services in the early 1980s. Companies are being established at a slower rate than that of the early 1970s, and the character of those that have become profitable is changing—perhaps the more significant factor. The emphasis seems to be shifting to specialized information services rather than computerized literature searching and document delivery. Trends indicate more database production, automated cataloging and indexing, publishing, and consulting.

The authors hope that this study will be informative for those already in the field, their potential clients, and those who wish to enter the industry to emulate its activities in the field of librarianship, where fees have only recently been charged.

ACKNOWLEDGMENTS

The authors would like to thank all the respondents to the survey of *Fee-Based Information Services* and are especially grateful to those who granted personal interviews and on-site visits. Also appreciated is the kind assistance of Kelly Warnken of Information Alternative and editor of the *Directory* and *Journal of Fee-Based Information Services,* who supplied listings of services, and Martin S. White, European Director, Creative Strategies International of London, England, who provided information regarding fee-based information services in the United Kingdom. The authors gratefully acknowledge the following fee-based information services for permission to reprint illustrative material in this book: Associated Information Managers; Documentation Associates; FIND/SVP; INFO-MART; INFO/MOTION; INFO-SEARCH; Inform (Minneapolis Public Library and Information Center); Information Associates Ltd., INFORMATION ON DEMAND; Information Specialists, Inc.; The Information Retriever, Inc.; INFORMATRON; Library Reports and Research Service, Inc.; NPM Information Services; Northwest Information Enterprises; Packaged Facts, Inc.; Regional Information & Communication Exchange (R.I.C.E.); TechSearch; Warner-Eddison Associates, Inc.; and Washington Researchers.

1

SURVEYING A GROWING FIELD

Fee-based information services, also known by other titles, have experienced a rapid growth rate in the United States since the mid-1970s. This relatively new industry originated in the late 1960s and began to develop in the early 1970s. Independent information specialists (free-lance librarians, information brokers, information consultants, and others) are entering the field at such a rapid pace that it is difficult to keep directory listings from becoming outdated. There are approximately 300 currently active services, many of which are not listed in the two directories on the market. In 1980, 36 states, 5 Canadian provinces, and 9 European countries had fee-based information services.

STUDY OF FEE-BASED INFORMATION SERVICES

This study is based upon 105 responses to a mail survey of fee-based information services conducted by the authors in the fall of 1979. The survey was supplemented by personal interviews and on-site visits during July and December of that year. The majority of the services surveyed were identified through the two directories that include most of the listings of companies in this field—*Information Market Place 1978–1979* (Bowker, 1978)[1] and the *Directory of Fee-Based Information Services* (2nd edition, *Information Alternative*, 1978). Services listed in volume one (1979) of the bimonthly *Journal of Fee-Based Information Services*,[2] which updates the directory, were also surveyed, as were some services known to the authors independently.

More than 80 listings of fee-based information services in North America and Europe were obtained from *Information Market Place 1978–1979,* which includes a variety of information products and services, from the section headed "Information Brokers." The *Directory* and *Journal of Fee-Based Information Services* provided listings for more than 290 services in 36 states, 5 Canadian provinces, the Virgin Islands, Australia, and England. (However, this number included those individuals that provide part-time or limited services. For example, more than 50 entries were for individuals who provide only indexing or abstracting services.)

In all, 326 survey forms were mailed and 188 were returned. Of those, 55 were disqualified because the individuals or companies were engaged only in indexing, editing, library consulting, database production, part-time free-lancing, and the like, and 25 wrote that they were no longer in business. The remainder (138) did not respond; nearly 50 percent of those included indexers or other part-time free-lancers, such as professors and retired librarians.

Survey Criteria

Because both information service directories exhibit differing views concerning the scope and definition of information services, the authors of this book had to set criteria for their study. A company or individual must provide a wide range of information services and products, including a combination of three or more of the following:

analytical reports
bibliographies
cataloging
consulting
database design and implementation
document delivery
management records
indexing
information-on-demand
library planning
manual searching
on-line searching
research
vocabulary/thesaurus building

The companies in this study were examined in terms of size, services offered, pricing and marketing strategies, and other pertinent factors such as background and training of staff and clientele. Respondents were asked to comment on their views of the future of the industry and on their competition. (A copy of the survey form is shown in Appendix 1.)

The intent here is to present an overview of fee-based information services. Since very little has been published on this segment of the information industry, this study examines the characteristics and diversity of fee-based information services. These range from large organizations and medium-sized companies to individual operations and those services backed by larger corporations. Seven categories were selected for analysis:

1. Large information services (those with more than 25 employees).
2. Medium-sized companies (more than 5 but fewer than 25 employees).
3. Small companies (fewer than 5 employees).
4. Independent brokers/freelancers.
5. Not-for-profit organizations.
6. Canadian services.
7. Information services within larger organizations (internal services).

Tables 1 and 2 show the geographical distribution of information services and respondents in each category in the United States and Canada.

An Industry in Search of a Name

Since no one title has universal support from all companies and individuals in the field, the authors selected "fee-based information services," preferred by almost all of the services with more than five employees. A fee-based information service is defined as an organization that undertakes research and provides information on demand for a fee. The principal focus in this book is on the for-profit sector of the industry. It should be noted, however, that several nonprofit organizations operate fee-based information services, and they, as well as "charge-back" internal services of large corporations, were included in the study.

During the late 1960s and early 1970s, the term "information broker" was popular among companies and individuals. This title is still widely debated at professional gatherings, but is

TABLE 1   GEOGRAPHICAL DISTRIBUTION OF FEE-BASED
INFORMATION SERVICES IN THE UNITED STATES

State (listed by rank)	Large	Medium	Small	Free-lance	Non-profit	Internal Services	Total Listing
California	—	5	5	9	4	—	23
New York	3	2	4	6	3	2	20
Washington DC	1	3	1	2	—	—	7
Massachusetts	—	2	1	2	1	1	7
Colorado	—	1	3	2	1	—	7
Pennsylvania	—	—	1	3	1	—	5
Ohio	—	1	1	1	1.	—	4
Florida	—	—	—	1	2	—	3
Illinois	—	1	1	—	1	—	3
New Jersey	1	—	1	—	—	—	2
Michigan	—	—	1	—	1	—	2
New Mexico	—	—	1	—	1	—	2
Utah	—	1	—	1	—	—	2
Maryland	—	1	—	—	—	—	1
Arizona	—	—	1	—	—	—	1
Kansas	—	—	—	1	—	—	1
Missouri	—	—	—	1	—	—	1
Nevada	—	—	—	1	—	—	1
Vermont	—	—	—	1	—	—	1
Oregon	—	—	—	1	—	—	1
Connecticut	—	—	—	—	1	—	1
Iowa	—	—	—	—	1	—	1
Texas	—	—	—	—	1	—	1
22 states	5	17	21	32	19	3	97

TABLE 2   GEOGRAPHICAL DISTRIBUTION OF FEE-BASED
INFORMATION SERVICES IN CANADA

Province	Medium	Small	Free-lance	Non-Profit	Total Listing
Alberta	1	—	—	1	2
British Columbia	—	—	1	—	1
Ontario	1	2	2	—	5
3 provinces	2	2	3	1	8

Note: Total survey responses in U.S. (Table 1) and Canada (Table 2) equals 105.

declining in popularity. According to Webster, a broker is "one who, for a commission or fee, brings parties together and assists in negotiating contracts between them." The term is appropriate since the information broker acts as the interface between the client and the source of information, and charges for the service. But many of those who responded to the survey indicated other preferences, such as information specialist, information scientist, free-lance librarian, free-lance specialist, library consultant, information professional, and information retailer.

There is a fine line between an information specialist and a consultant. The first provides information-gathering services and the second provides evaluation and analysis. It can be argued, however, that in order to gather and package information, the specialist must often utilize evaluative techniques and is, thus, working in a consulting capacity. Interesting enough, in the United Kingdom, brokering, or "broking," connotes real estate transactions only, and the common terms are "information consultancy" and "on-demand information services." Personal contact between the client and the information specialist is paramount to the success of any information service. It is also crucial, since the bulk of the activity of a fee-based information service is in its repeat business.

HISTORY OF FEE-BASED INFORMATION SERVICES

As indicated by the survey replies, fee-based information services have experienced four periods of development (see Table 3). Those formed prior to 1950 were generally products of mission-oriented research in science or technology, often in academic institutions. Examples are two nonprofit organizations—the Engineering Societies Library in New York City, founded in 1913 to serve the informational needs of engineering professionals, and the University of New Mexico's Bureau of Business and Economic Research, formed in 1945 to provide business, economic, and demographical information for the university as well as to private organizations. In 1958, one of the largest information services was established in New York City. World Wide Information Services began primarily as a specialized commercial news service for journalists. One respondent to the survey indicated a business start four years earlier (in 1954) as a free-lance specialist and consultant. During the 1960s, information services greatly increased in number as a response to industry

TABLE 3   HISTORY OF FEE-BASED INFORMATION SERVICES

| Category | *Founding Dates* | | | |
	Pre-1950	1950s	1960s	1970s
Large Companies	—	1	2	2
Medium-Sized Companies	—	—	2	15
Small Companies	—	—	2	19
Free-lancers	—	1	4	27
Canadian	—	—	1	6
Not-For-Profit	2	—	9	9
Services Within Large Companies	—	—	—	3
Total	2	2	20	81

Note: One Canadian information service was added to the "Not-for-Profit" category and was not included in the "Canadian" grouping.

needs. Twenty fee-based information services were established during that decade, nine of which are nonprofit. In the 1970s, the largest crop of information services appeared; 81 respondents indicated starting dates during the 1970s, with clusters of services formed in the years 1973–1975 and 1977–1979. One of the larger services, FIND, was incorporated in 1969, but did not begin operation as it is now known until 1972.

A large majority of the free-lancers who established themselves in the early 1970s were products of the grass-roots "alternatives to librarianship" movement, which originated on the West Coast, especially in the San Francisco Bay Area. The mid-1960s were a turning point for several others who had been introduced to information science in schools of library science. On-line information retrieval was integrated into library school curricula, with the main activity coming from the University of California at Berkeley and Syracuse University in upstate New York. A workshop entitled "The Information Broker/Freelance Librarian," held April 3, 1976, at Syracuse University School of Information Studies as a continuing education program, brought together information specialists, special librarians, and aspiring students. One student formed INFO/MOTION in Massachusetts that same year.

Seminars and workshops on the topic of providing information free or for a fee are still drawing crowds. An institute sponsored by the Library Association of the City University of New York (LACUNY), entitled "The Information Industry and the Library—Competition or Cooperation," was held April 16, 1979, and attracted more than 400 information professionals and spokespersons as well as librarians and students.[3] Susan Klement of Information Resources, Toronto, presents "Alternatives in Librarianship Workshops" and has participated in seminars given at American library schools. In her promotional literature, Klement states that the workshops "seek to broaden the horizons of librarianship, not to suggest alternatives to the profession . . . the workshops encourage participants to view their profession with new insight and enthusiasm and to have greater respect for their own abilities."[4] Various aspects of promoting information services—marketing, client-consultant relationship, information as a commodity, fee-for service—are discussed, and personnel from small nonprofit information firms, large for-profit information companies, public or academic fee-for-service departments, and "alternative" librarians appear on panels. Library schools have offered continuing education programs on the topic, and a 1979 "Critical Issues Conference" at Pratt Institute in New York City featured a three-day symposium on information marketing. Cassettes of the conference are marketed separately, with the sales indicating a high interest from the library community.[5]

Kelly Warnken, of Information Alternative and editor of the *Directory of Fee-Based Information Services,* has encouraged seminars and workshops on a national scale. Through her publications, she attempts to disseminate information for brokers and to publicize the fee-based information service industry. The far-reaching effects of these publications are difficult to determine. Several information services hear about the publications only through word-of-mouth and are only too happy to be listed at no cost. Many of the respondents who were interviewed in this survey commented that although listings in the directory might not generate new business, they are invaluable for making the firms aware of colleagues, competitors, similar organizations, or potential subcontracting agreements. This information cannot be gleaned from telephone listings in the Yellow Pages because only a small percentage of the information services advertise there. Moreover, since there are no headings for Information Services, such companies are listed under Library and Information Services, Market Research and Analysis, or Research Services.

The most valuable information trading occurs at professional meetings, institutes, and conferences. This does not necessarily bring key people together, however, because many information service principals and employees belong to a variety of professional associations. The logical choice might be the Information Industry Association (IIA) and its subgroup, Associated Information Managers (AIM). IIA was founded in 1967 to promote the development of private enterprise in the information industry. It is a trade association of more than 150 corporate members— for-profit organizations and individuals engaged in the development or application of advanced technology to meet the information needs of various markets. The IIA lobbies on behalf of its membership for the development of national and international information policies. The purpose of AIM, which began operation in 1978, is "to promote the concept of coordinated professional management of an organization's total information resource, and to aid the professional development of the manager performing this task."[6]

It is interesting, and perhaps indicative of the difficulty in trading information, to note that of the 105 services that responded to the survey, only 19 belong to AIM, 11 to IIA, and 5 to both organizations. (Table 4 indicates professional association memberships of information services.) The Special Libraries Association (SLA) has the highest number of memberships from the information service industry, suggesting that most of the services are run by special librarians (in fact, 65 of the 105 principals have library science degrees).

Since no one professional association acts as the forum for fee-based information services, memberships are quite diverse. On the West Coast, especially in the San Francisco Bay Area, such groups as Women Library Workers and Women Entrepreneurs have a popular following. Several information specialists in the survey expressed concern over the need for a universal professional title as well as a forum for this sector of the industry. Both would serve to heighten group recognition and raise user consciousness on national and international levels. Those interviewed also commented on the lack of professional standards or ethics and the need for quality control. A splinter group of AIM, the Ad Hoc Committee of Information Brokers, met at the National Information Conference and Exhibition (NICE III, sponsored by IIA) in 1979 to discuss their concerns. An informal liaison was established among members of this group, and the intent of future meetings will be to establish a distinct division

TABLE 4 PROFESSIONAL ASSOCIATION MEMBERSHIPS

Association	Big 5	Medium	Small	Free-Lance	Non-Profit	Canadian	Internal Services	Total
IIA	2	5		1	1	1	1	11
AIM	2	6	4	4	1	1	1	19
ASIS	—	7	10	7	12	4	1	41
SLA	—	8	13	13	12	5	2	53
ALA	—	5	4	13	13	2	—	37
Mgt./Mkg. (AMA, SBA)	1	3	1	3	—	—	—	8
ASIDIC	—	1	—	—	2	—	—	3
On-line User Groups	—	—	1	—	3	—	—	4
Other (state, regional library associations)	—	14	11	17	8	5	—	55
None	1	2	4	1	3	1	—	12

Note: Fifty-three information services indicated memberships in more than one professional association; the Canadian nonprofit organization was included with the "Canadian" group.

for the information service sector, complete with professional ethics, guidelines, and public relations programs. In their search for a name and identity, fee-based information services must maintain their informal and formal networks and establish group solidarity on an international level. Several of the British services expressed the wish for reciprocity with American firms. Many services in the United States already have established foreign information exchanges.

There has been much speculation regarding the future of the fee-based information service industry (discussed in detail in Chapter 11). A few of the pioneers have grown into successful business enterprises, creating models for others in the field and for aspirants. As evidenced by the authors' study, information services in the private and public sectors will continue to prosper, with the larger organizations dominating the market. Annual revenue for any of the larger information services is in excess of $1 million. FIND, for example, reported annual revenues for 1980 in excess of $3 million.[7] Although some believe that information conglomerates will emerge during the 1980s, with larger firms "swallowing up" smaller operations, Andrew Garvin, president of FIND, is convinced that "there will always be a market for free-lance research and contract-on-demand research." Indeed, the market is large, and a fee-based information service with the right ingredients of marketing, management, and money has the potential for success.

The idea of charging for information services is slowly evolving in libraries, and it is expected that many more public and academic libraries will develop services along the lines of Cleveland Public Library's Facts for a Fee, Dallas Public Library's Custom Research Service, and Minneapolis Public Library's Inform. As budgets become more restrictive, libraries may implement a charge system or apply for state or federal funding to provide subsidized information services. On-line bibliographic retrieval services will also change to accommodate the needs of information clientele. Where once the information specialist's duty was to act as an intermediary (search strategist, for example), soon the client will be able to access databases directly. In this event, the role of the information specialist will be expanded to provide additional evaluative and analytical services. Information specialists view information as a resource—one that can be tapped, capitalized, or expensed. Information as a commodity and a profitable good is the underlying philosophy of the industry. A variation on this theme is offered by some in the field—information is free and one does not charge for information per se; the charge is for the service of repackaging or reformatting the data.

The following chapters highlight the major components of fee-based information services. An overview of the industry, based on survey results, will provide the background for the chapters on marketing and information-gathering techniques. Some of the major fee-based information services will be spotlighted. The international scene will be discussed with primary focus on England. Independent information specialists, the information brokers, will be examined as a phenomenon and individually. An analysis of the economics of fee-based information services, as well as the impact on the future for libraries and librarianship, will provide realistic forecasts for the industry as a whole. A detailed listing of fee-based information services in the United States and Canada is found in Appendix 3. It is the authors' intent to provide a conclusive study of this emerging industry that will lead the way for future reviews. This state-of-the-art report will be useful for existing information services, potential users, students, and other interested information professionals. For those entering the field of fee-based information service, this study will spotlight some of the pitfalls encountered by the industry pioneers.

BASIC QUESTIONS AND ANSWERS

Q. What is a fee-based information service?

A. An organization that undertakes research and provides information on demand for a charge.

Q. How many fee-based information services are in operation in the United States?

A. Approximately 300.

Q. What directories list most of the fee-based information services?

A. *Information Industry Market Place* and *Directory of Fee-Based Information Services.*

Q. What kinds of fee-based information services are in operation in the United States?

A. There are six different categories: large (more than 25 employees), medium-sized (5–25), small (fewer than 5), freelance, nonprofit, and internal (within larger organizations).

Q. Is this industry confined to the United States?

A. No, there are fee-based information services in Canada and in Great Britain and other European countries.

NOTES

1. The second edition of *Information Market Place,* publication November 1980, is entitled *Information Industry Market Place 1980* and contains over 120 listings of fee-based information services. This book is marketed in Europe as *Information Trade Directory.*
2. First published in 1976, the *Directory of Fee-Based Information Services* is now in its third edition and contains some 300 listings. A fourth edition is scheduled for January 1981. Listings in the second (1978) and third (1980) edition have been updated by volumes one (1979) and two (1980) of the *Journal of Fee-Based Information Services.* However, supplements updating the upcoming fourth edition of the directory may be issued separately from the journal (from Kelly Warnken, Directory editor).
3. "Information Entrepreneurs Stake Claims at LACUNY," *Library Journal* 104 (June 1, 1979): 1199.
4. Information Resources promotional brochure.
5. Cassettes are available from Information Yield, 311 Stonecrest Dr., Dewitt, NY 13214.
6. Associated Information Managers roster, 1979–1980, p. 7.
7. Personal Communication.

2

AN OVERVIEW OF FEE-BASED INFORMATION SERVICES

This overview of fee-based information services stems from data supplied by the 105 organizations that responded positively to the survey conducted by the authors in 1979 (see Chapter 1 in the section, Study of Fee-Based Information Services). As noted in Chapter 1, the fee-based information service industry can be divided into large, medium-sized, small, and nonprofit concerns. With the addition of the Canadian market, these are the divisions detailed in this chapter.

LARGE INFORMATION SERVICES

"Large" is a relative term in regard to fee-based information services because no service as yet has grown beyond the small business category. Only five corporations in the field employ more than 25 full-time staff. In common with virtually all businesses and individuals in the field, they are experiencing rapid growth.

The five largest information service companies that responded to the survey are FIND/SVP, Washington Researchers, Environment Information Center, TCR Service, Inc., and World Wide Information Services. They are representative of the large companies in this field.

One of the five (World Wide) was founded in 1958, and the youngest (Environment Information) was established in 1975.

Three are in New York City (TCR is in nearby Englewood Cliffs, New Jersey), yet Washington Researchers, in Washington, D.C., appears to have more clients in New York than in its home community.

The firms were founded by people with backgrounds in journalism, law, and business administration (M.B.A. training), and are generally staffed by subject specialists rather than librarians. Only one has a high percentage of degreed librarians on its staff (35 percent).

The companies and their principals are active (see Table 4 in Chapter 1) in the Information Industry Association (IIA), the American Marketing Association (AMA), the U.S. Trademark Association, and the North American Society for Corporate Planning. The number and range of association memberships are far more limited than for the group of information services that employ 5 to 25 persons.

Two of the firms specialize, one in trademark services and the other in energy and environmental information. All five have a broad range of services. They perform information-on-demand, document delivery, on-line searching, and extended research. All do consulting and are active as publishers; four do analytical reports as well as research. Three prepare bibliographies, conduct seminars, and provide indexing services; three produce market reports and two provide selective dissemination of information (SDI) services. Only one offers translation services.

Large corporations are the primary clientele of the large information services. For two of them, large corporations represent over 80 percent of the total volume of business, and for only one is it less than 50 percent. One service does half of its work for small businesses, which comprise less than 20 percent of clients for the others. Government is not an important source of revenue; one of the specialized firms gets about 25 percent of its business in this way; the percentage is much less for the others. This is in sharp contrast with the pattern of information services with fewer than 25 employees.

The not-for-profit sector is also not a major revenue source. Only one of the firms, which has a specialized service, reports a high percentage (40) of requests from academic institutions. One of the firms that specializes obtains 30 percent of its business from the legal profession.

Repeat business is higher for this group than for any other of the information services. The companies report that from 80 to 95 percent of their clients have dealt with them previously. New

York City is the principal location for clients, with up to one-third of the requests generated there. But all of these services have clients throughout the United States, and two have substantial international business.

Marketing departments of corporations are the clients most often served by these larger information services, and the percentages range as high as 70 and 80 for two of the firms. Research and development departments are second in importance, but only one service reports as much as 20 percent of its requests from such personnel. Top administration accounts for a very small percentage of requests.

Direct access by the person seeking the information, rather than access through an intermediary, is widespread. The larger services use a variety of promotional tools, including Yellow Pages advertising (2), professional journal ads (2), direct mail (5), conference attendance and exhibitions (4), seminars (4), sales calls (3), distribution of their own publications (3), and news stories (3). All agree, however, that the most important sources of new clients are word-of-mouth and client referral. One of the respondents regards conference attendance and exhibits as the most effective tool for supplementing word-of-mouth. One prefers sales calls, and another elects special introductory rates. All consider direct mail to be minimally effective.

The sources of information used to answer a client's question are diverse. Each service lists a first choice source—in no case a nearby library. One relies almost exclusively on an in-house collection; the others report figures as low as 5 percent utilization for that source. Another calls experts on the telephone for nearly 95 percent of its data gathering. Three rely heavily on in-house or proprietary databases, and all do on-line searching of remote databases. In one case, the service obtains 30 percent of its information by searching commercial databases.

Most customers of the larger information services deal through telephone or by mail. Only two services have as many as 5 percent of their clients coming in person. Two have more than 70 percent of the requests via mail; another two list 90 percent via telephone. The markedly different patterns seem to reflect the preferences of the individual services rather than those of the clients.

Pricing structures vary, but services are generally calculated by the hour and run as high as $75 per hour for professional research work. Three of the companies reported that they selected their pricing strategy to assure an adequate profit margin and to remain competitive. These same firms seek subscriptions or retainers for quick reference services, and two bill by the job; four bill by the job for research undertaken. One firm uses both of these approaches plus billing clients in advance; three give free telephone tips or referrals, but two do not offer free services at all.

One of the larger information services claims no competition; of the four who identified competitors, only one named a firm from among the largest five. Only one competitor from among the small information services was identified by name. The competition appears to be in specific areas of activity rather than across the board, with computer searching and document delivery the most common areas. Moreover, competition is perceived as national rather than local.

Legal liability is generally rejected, although one firm clearly states that it considers itself liable for the work it does, but not for the accuracy of the sources it uses. It does not double-check all sources.

There seem to be no formal mechanisms for evaluating company performance. A high volume of repeat business is generally considered evidence of good work, but one service monitors complaints as a way of assessing performance.

No reliable data is available regarding turnaround time since the nature of the requests received by each firm is so varied. All report ranges from one or two days to a month or more.

These larger companies are optimistic about future growth for the information service industry, but they have different expectations for their own futures. One of the principals feels that growth in the industry might be at the expense of some of the smaller services. Although there will always be a market for the free-lance researcher, he feels that there may be a shakedown among corporations in the field. Another observes that greater development of information services within client companies will affect the potential growth for the entire fee-based information service industry.

MEDIUM-SIZED INFORMATION SERVICES

The medium-sized information services that were surveyed display some common characteristics, as do the larger concerns. Of the 17 respondents (see list at the end of this section) in this category, all but 2 were founded in the 1970s. There is a definite pattern in the years 1971–1974; five companies were established in 1973 alone. These services are located in large metropolitan areas in California (5), New York (3), Washington, D.C. (4), Colorado (1), Illinois (1), Ohio (1), Massachusetts (1), and Utah (1).

The initial amount of capital needed to launch the medium-sized firms varied: more than $100,000 (reported by one), less than $100,000 (6), less than $10,000 (8), and less than $1,000 (reported by one). Seven services have staffs in the 5–10 person category; others indicate staffs of 10–15 (four services) and 15–20 (five services). One has a staff of 20–25.

An interesting characteristic of medium-sized fee-based information services is the high number of degreed librarians on staff as opposed to the low number employed by the larger companies. Five (including three sole proprietorships) report staffs of 80–100 percent degreed librarians. Other areas of background and training include library automation, information retrieval, systems design and analysis, and records management. Nine have staff with training and experience in the library field and six in other backgrounds, including business, journalism, arts/music, and engineering.

This group appears more active in library and information science associations than the larger companies. Memberships include IIA, and its subgroup, the Association of Information Managers (AIM), the Special Libraries Association (SLA), the American Society for Information Science (ASIS), and the American Library Association (ALA), as well as local and regional library and business groups. In addition, the services also named the American Records Managers Association, the National Micrographics Association, the American Marketing Association, the Newsletter Association of America, American Chemical Society, Association of Professional Genealogists, and Women Entrepreneurs.

The primary services offered by medium-sized information companies are document delivery (16), research (15), consulting (14), information-on-demand (12), and conducting seminars (10). Additional services include records management, software development, systems analysis and design, space planning, and computerized indexing and abstracting. Very few are involved with publishing and/or translating activities. Seven offer total subject coverage; five focus exclusively on business; two provide government information; and one each specializes in the humanities and social sciences. There is a wide range of subject coverage in this group, with a trend toward specialization (such as solar energy, engineering, performing arts).

The clients of the medium-sized group are large corporations in the private sector (20 to 80 percent). Small business accounts for 20–60 percent; government 20–50 percent, and nonprofit organizations 5–15 percent. Only one corporation caters largely (90 percent) to government and nonprofit organizations. One sole proprietor states that although small companies account for a high percentage of business in terms of volume/sales, large corporations account for a higher percentage in terms of net revenue. Clients are primarily in research and development and marketing activities. One of the respondents, specializing in procuring federal documents, indicates 95 percent of its clientele from government. Two other corporations report half of their clientele involved with manufacturing. Lawyers, consultants, energy engineers, and performing artists make up good percentages of the clientele for some.

Information services in this group have a high percentage of repeat business, with a majority reporting rates between 50 and 75 percent. Two sole proprietorships indicate a 90 percent rate, although for one this figure is for document delivery services only. Inquiries are usually received directly for all but two sole proprietorships, who report only half of their inquiries in this way. Librarians are frequently the clients for at least one service.

All of the companies in this group name word-of-mouth as the most effective means of procuring business. Direct mail/informational brochures follow, with one service reporting that this strategy attracts 95 percent of its business. The majority have attractively designed and produced brochures, letterheads, business cards, and the like. Two replies stated that conducting seminars and exhibiting at conferences are as effective as word-of-mouth. One sole proprietor uses radio advertising on occasion.

Requests from clients average 100 per month for most of the companies. One sole proprietorship processes 8,000 document delivery requests per month, and one corporation handles 2,000 such requests per month. For two of the corporations, all requests are via telephone, and the majority report a 60–99 percent range for telephone requests and a 40–85 percent range for mail requests. One sole proprietorship receives 95 percent of its requests in person. There is a very low percentage of telex requests. Ten of the companies maintain records of how their requests are received, and one has an informal records system. Nearby libraries and on-line databases are used by most of these services more than half the time to answer inquiries. Additional sources such as government, distant libraries, staff expertise, and special agreements with foreign information services are also listed.

The price range varies in this group, but most prices are based on the cost plus a predetermined profit-margin system. Three respondents set their fees for document-delivery service based on competitors' rates. Research fees range from $25 to $50 per hour, with an average of $35 per hour. Some services offer more than one payment option for their clients, such as payment in advance (14) and subscription/retainer options (13). All have billing services; one stipulates that only subscribers to its research service are entitled to the quick-information service. Five offer free referral services.

Only four of this group did not know of other services or competitors, but 10 listed those they regarded as national competition, including both the larger and medium-sized services. Only one service (a genealogical research firm) assumes legal liability for the provision of accurate information. Most respondents feel that using secondary sources of information does not constitute liability; one company has a published disclaimer to this effect.

Client feedback and repeat business are the techniques most often used to evaluate effectiveness for these companies. Again, the only service with internal quality control is the genealogical research company.

Average turnaround varies greatly and depends on the nature of the services rendered. For document delivery, several have 24-hour service and, for research, the range is days to weeks to years. New planned services include publishing, management consulting, software developments, on-line applications, and electronic mail delivery.

Medium-sized information service respondents:
> Cibbarelli and Associates (Huntington Beach, Calif.)
> Dataflow Systems, Inc. (Bethesda, Md.)
> Documentation Associates (Santa Monica, Calif.)
> Editec (Chicago, Ill.)
> Facs, Inc. (Washington, D.C.)
> Judith Finell MusicServices, Inc. (N.Y.C.)
> Global Engineering Documentation Services, Inc. (Santa Ana, Calif.)
> Government Information Services (Washington, D.C.)
> Information for Business (N.Y.C. and Cambridge, Mass.)

Information Management Specialists (Denver, Colo.)
INFORMATION ON DEMAND (Berkeley, Calif.)
Information Specialists (Cleveland, Ohio)
INFORMATRON (Brooklyn, N.Y.)
Solar Energy Information Services (San Mateo, Calif.)
Warner-Eddison Associates, Inc. (Cambridge, Mass.)
Washington Representative Services (Washington, D.C.)
Western Consultants (Bountiful, Utah)

SMALL COMMERCIAL SERVICES

Twenty-one small information services—fewer than five full-time employees—were identified in the survey (see list at end of this section). The companies were founded from 1962 through 1979 (two were established before 1972 and eight in 1979). Eleven are incorporated, five are sole proprietorships, and five are partnerships. One is actually an internal information service of a corporation, which is seeking to extend its clientele beyond the parent company.

The smaller information services are almost all located near major metropolitan areas, such as New York and Washington, D.C., and somewhat smaller areas such as Albuquerque, New Mexico; Boulder, Colorado; Columbus, Ohio; and Palo Alto, California. Their initial capitalization was generally under $1,000 (five reported up to $10,000, and one reported more than $10,000).

Seventeen of those surveyed retain staffs of 1–5 persons. The others are staffed by the head of the service alone, sometimes with part-time aid. Almost all the people who head these services, as well as the full-time staff, have backgrounds in librarianship, although advanced degrees in other fields are common too.

The names under which these organizations operate vary: information service (6), information specialist (4), information manager (4), information broker (3), library consultant (2), information retailer (1), information research company (1), photo library (1), free-lance librarian (1) and visual picture research service (1). They are members of such professional organizations as SLA, ASIS, ALA, AIM, American Society for Picture Professionals, Canadian Association for Information Science, and American Chemical Society.

All of the services perform manual searches, and 13 offer

on-line searching. Other activities include preparing bibliographies (19), information-on-demand (18), consulting (17), SDI (14), and document delivery (15). Research and indexing are listed by 14 of the services, but only 7 develop market reports and 6 do analytical reports. Other infrequently offered services are presentation of seminars (7), translation (5), thesaurus development (1), and records management (1). The subject areas are most often business (19) and science/technology (18). Eleven companies give complete coverage, 16 offer social science services, 15 list health sciences, and 14 indicate humanities.

Small business is most often the client to the small service, although two report 75 percent and three indicate more than 50 percent of their business with large corporations. Other listed clientele are government agencies (20 percent of the total for four firms, and more than 50 percent for one); nonprofit organizations (not a significant source of business for most, but one highly specialized sci-tech firm receives 50 percent of its requests from academic and public libraries); and individuals (six firms, 30 percent of the total volume for one).

The geographical distribution of clientele is generally narrower for small firms than for larger information services, with most doing more than 80 percent of all business within the state in which they are located. Three firms do more than half of their business on the national level, one as much as 75 percent. Only one has a substantial international clientele.

The activities of the clients are quite diverse. Research and development are mentioned as often as marketing, with seven firms getting half or more of their requests from this sector. Administration, production, exploration, publishing, and editing divisions of client companies were also mentioned. Almost all of the firms have 90 to 100 percent direct contact with their clients, but four indicate half or more of their clients operating through other parties.

The level of repeat business varies from firm to firm. Since there is no correlation between the age or size of the company and the level of repeat business, perceived performance may be the main factor.

These small companies differ in their opinion of the best marketing approach—14 cite word-of-mouth, 7 direct mail, which is the most widely used technique (18 firms). Although 6 have used newspaper advertising, none say it is a highly effective medium. Also mentioned are Yellow Page advertising (7, with 2 naming it as most effective); professional journal advertising (8, with one placing it among the most effective); conferences and meetings (3 of the 15 who attended conferences consider them quite effective); and sales calls (one of 8 finds this as an effective technique).

The average number of monthly requests ranges from one to 200, and no describable pattern is evident because the nature of the requests is so varied.

On-line databases are the most popular source of information—5 companies use them more than 50 percent of the time to answer queries. One information service recovers 95 percent of the needed information through computer searching. In-house collections are a minor source for 18 firms, but the other 3 use their own collections from 80 to 95 percent of the time. Nearby libraries are used extensively by half the small information services, although only 5 use them more than 75 percent of the time. Only one respondent experienced any restrictions or fees in using nearby libraries. Telephoning experts is not a popular information-gathering technique, but 4 firms use it 25–30 percent of the time.

Requests are usually received by telephone, but seven firms get half or more in the mail and three often receive 80–100 percent of all requests by mail. In-person queries are rare, but two services receive 60 and 85 percent of requests this way.

Cost plus a predetermined profit margin is the principal pricing strategy of 7 firms; 5 set their fees based on competitors' charges; and 9 use negotiated fees. Only one firm reported actually surveying the prices of others in order to set its own prices. A large minority would not quote specific fees; those that did so generally quoted $25–$30 per hour, compared with the $75 per hour that is common among the larger information services. Only 2 firms collect fees in advance, but 17 collect by billing for each completed job. The 4 who use a subscription program generally limit its use to quick information. Only 6 of the firms give occasional free information. One company provides deposit accounts for its clients.

Most of these firms know of others who offer similar services, but eight do not consider other firms as competitors, and only five think the competition is significant. Virtually all view competition as national rather than local or regional. One firm among the five largest was mentioned as a competitor, and three firms in the middle-sized group were listed.

None of the small services assume legal liability for the accuracy of information they provide, but several also admitted that they had not thought about the matter. The work contract for one specifically states that the service will not assume liability for inaccurate information.

Almost all these small companies measure effectiveness of their services by looking at repeat business rates or noting referrals. Only one uses formal evaluation forms. One firm described a reciprocal agreement among members of a specialized association (picture researchers) whereby problem-solving techniques were exchanged. Most of these firms plan no new services in the near future, but one is contemplating newsletter or directory publishing, another book publishing, and another "production of materials." One also wishes to expand and install facsimile transfer facilities.

The prognosis for the industry as a whole was described in glowing terms by these companies. One sees increasing competition from libraries in the area of computer searching, and another forecasts displacement by larger companies with substantial computer facilities. Independent contracting for specialized or mission-oriented research and information may be a growing area.

Small information service respondents:

      Access Innovations, Inc. (Albuquerque, N.Mex.)

      After-Image (Los Angeles, Calif.)

      Bogart-Brociner Associates (Annapolis, Md.)

      Carol Mae S. Campion (Scranton, Pa.)

      Chemica Data Center (Columbus, Ohio)

      The Diversified Finders (Long Beach, Calif.)

      Geoscience Information Service (Chico, Calif.)

      Infocorp (Chicago, Ill.)

      Information Associates Ltd. (Tucson, Ariz.)

      Information Resources (Winthrop, Mass.)

      The Information Retriever (Denver, Colo.)

      INFO-SEARCH (Bloomfield Hills, Mich.)

      The Information Store (San Francisco, Calif.)

      Library Reports and Research Services (Denver, Colo.)

      MBP/Information Research (Bergenfield, N.J.)

      Marshe Infoservices, Inc. (Wantagh, N.Y.)

      Packaged Facts (N.Y.C.)

      Picture Research (Washington, D.C.)

      Savage Information Services (Rancho Palo Verdes, Calif.)

Technical Library Service (N.Y.C.)
TechSearch (Denver, Colo.)

THE NONPROFIT SECTOR

A number of nonprofit organizations offer information services (see list of survey respondents at the end of this section). The oldest began in 1961 and more than half started in 1975 or earlier. Initial capital outlay was generally under $10,000, but at least 2 companies were launched with more than $1 million each.

Nineteen of these nonprofit services have staffs of more than one person, with two firms employing more than 50 persons, one between 25 and 50, one between 10 and 15, and four between 5 and 10. The staff members generally have both subject and library degrees, and a large percentage have library experience as well. Nine describe themselves as information services, two as information brokers, and eight as information specialists. The other terms used are library exchange service and technology transfer brokers.

These nonprofit organizations are members of such groups as ALA, ASIS, SLA, IIA. On-line searching and the preparation of bibliographies are the most widely offered services; 16 offer each. Fifteen offer manual searching and 14 provide information-on-demand.

The most effective marketing stimuli for generating business are: word-of-mouth (12); direct mail (17, with 6 listing it as their most effective medium); conference and institute attendance (4 consider it the best way of generating new business); publications (3 of 10 who issue publications consider it the best marketing tool in addition to one of the above); seminars (8, 2 of whom regard it as among the most effective techniques for obtaining new clients); specialized publications (7 have coverage, but none traces new business to that fact). Other techniques are seldom used by this group.

The number of requests per month for information services is substantially higher than that for commercial information firms—as high as 119,000 requests per month for one professional society, which provides reference service to thousands of its members throughout the country. Most of the others report from 200 to 2,000 requests monthly, but two have from 4,500 to 6,000 per month and one reports an average of only 4 requests per month.

In-house collections are a major source of information for the nonprofit services; eight list more than 75 percent of their information as coming from there. On-line databases are also used heavily, more than 70 percent for four of the services. Nearby libraries are infrequently consulted; only two services rely on them more than 10 percent of the time. Four services report some restriction in using these libraries, primarily restrictions imposed on everyone—noncirculating materials, limited hours, membership fees, and so on. Telephoning experts is frequently 10 percent of the total, but the use of other information services is apparently rare.

There is a high incidence of in-person use by clients. Three services say that over 95 percent of their requests are received in this manner, and four list figures from 25–60 percent. Mail requests are generally less than 50 percent for all except five of the services; one receives only mail requests. Telephone requests amount to more than 50 percent for six services.

Cost represents the basis for setting fees. The most common professional research rates are $25 and $30 per hour, but some services do offer a lower rate. Most quick information service is billed by the job, but monthly billings are common among nonprofit information services as are departmental accounts within the same organization. Only two organizations bill in advance and two accept retainers. Research services are billed in the same manner. One provides a quarter-hour billing rate. Free services are fairly common; 13 of the respondents offer, in particular, quick reference and short consultations over the phone. Eight of these nonprofit groups could not identify similar information services, but the others named a wide variety of commercial and nonprofit services. Six nonprofit information services consider those named to be competitors. The competition is more generally seen as regional rather than national, but three services regard competition as international.

Two nonprofit services accept legal liability for the accuracy of their research. Repeat business and client feedback are the principal means of measuring the effectiveness of the services, but in-house reviews are used by two and surveys are periodically carried out by three others. Turnaround time is generally fast, often less than a day. This might be due to the rather large number of in-person queries that many of these services receive.

Nonprofit information service respondents:

> Alberta Information Retrieval Association (Edmonton, Alberta)

Biological Information Service (Riverside, Calif.)

Bureau of Business and Economic Research/University of New Mexico (Albuquerque)

Business Information Center of Golden Gate University (San Francisco, Calif.)

Colorado Technical Reference Center (Boulder, Colo.)

Computer Search Center IITRI (Chicago, Ill.)

Engineering Societies Library (N.Y.C.)

FSU Search (Florida State University, Tallahassee)

Facts for a Fee (Cleveland Public Library, Ohio)

Franklin Research Center/SISO (Philadelphia, Pa.)

ILR: Access (Cornell University, Ithaca, N.Y.)

Inform (Minneapolis, Minn.)

MIT Computerized Literature Search Service (Mass.)

National Investment Library (N.Y.C.)

NERAC (University of Connecticut, Storrs)

Rare-Earth Information Center (Ames, Iowa)

Regional Information and Communication Exchange (Rice University, Houston, Tex.)

Science Book and Serial Exchange (Ann Arbor, Mich.)

Text Information Processing Services (Gainesville, Fla.)

World Trade Information Center (N.Y.C.)

Women's Educational Equity Communications Network (San Francisco, Calif.)

CANADIAN SERVICES

Seven Canadian fee-based information services responded to the survey—Canadatum, Infomart, Information Resources, and Dean Tudor of Toronto; Michael A. Dagg Associates of Ottawa; ISI Infosearch, Inc. of Vancouver; and Schick Information Systems, Ltd. of Edmonton. The oldest was established in 1969 and the youngest in 1979. Two are corporations, two are partnerships, and three are sole proprietorships. Capitalization was modest—less than $1,000 for three, no more than $10,000 for all but one of the rest. The exception is a corporation subsidiary that committed well over $100,000. Its primary service is now the marketing of databases.

Three Canadian services have no employees other than the head person. The rest employ fewer than 5, 5–10, and 25–50 persons. Subject degrees are more common than library degrees in three of the services, but two have solely library credentials and six of the seven principals have library degrees.

The seven respondents operate under various names; four use information service, and three use more than one designation—information broker, information specialist, free-lance librarian, library consultant, records management consultant, and librarian. They are active in such groups as SLA, ALA, IIA, ASIS, the Canadian Association for Information Science, and the Canadian Library Association.

The only service performed by all seven Canadian firms is the preparation of bibliographies. Other services include document delivery, information-on-demand, research and manual searching (6), on-line searching (4), and consulting and SDI services (5 for each). Four provide a variety of other services; only one offers translations, and none produce market reports. Five of the services cover all subject areas; one does not work in the health science field and another does not work in science/technology areas.

Small business makes up 20 to 60 percent of the clientele for four of the firms, and large corporations form 35 to 50 percent for the same group. Government is a major source for one, and nonprofit organizations represent 75 percent of business for another.

Repeat business is generally under 50 percent, although in two firms it is 80 and 100 percent. Virtually all of the activity is confined to the local or provincial area; one firm does 80 percent of its business internationally.

Marketing is not a major activity of the clients, but research and development are 70–90 percent of the three services' clientele. Other client groups are engaged in publishing, public relations, and administrative or association offices. Clients have direct access to the services—100 percent for five services and 90 percent for the remaining two.

Word-of-mouth seems to be the most effective means of attracting new business in Canada as it is with U.S. information services. Other activities include sales calls (four of the five users consider them highly effective), attendance at conferences and professional meetings (considered by two as a very effective way of meeting prospective clients), and direct mail (called very effective by one of the three who use it). None have tried Yellow Pages advertising or radio commercials, but three firms have placed advertisements in professional journals and two in newspapers.

Requests to these companies range from 5 to 15 per month. The principal sources for answering requests are nearby libraries (one of the services uses them 50 percent of the time and two use them 80 percent), on-line database searching (two use them 90 and 100 percent), in-house collections (preferred by one), and telephoning of experts (two rely on them more than 20 percent of the time). The telephone is the most commonly used medium for the submission of queries—40–90 percent of the time for all but one service, which has a 90-percent in-person business.

Five Canadian firms set their fees on the basis of cost plus a predetermined profit margin, but four have negotiated fees. Rates vary from $15 to $50 per hour, with $25–30 per hour most common. All bill by the job for both quick information and research services. All but one offer some free services.

Five of these companies are aware of the other information services, but only three see them as competitors. Two view the competition as regional, and one views it on all levels. Six do not assume legal liability for the accuracy of the information they provide; three admitted they had not considered the issue very carefully.

Repeat business and client feedback are regarded as the most effective evaluative tools, with opinion divided as to which is the more important. Turnaround time ranges from 10 minutes to 10 months, but several firms try to offer same-day service when asked.

A newsletter, SDI services, and resumé preparation services are under consideration by a couple of these firms. Predictions for future growth are cautious but good.

BASIC QUESTIONS AND ANSWERS

Q. Which are some of the largest fee-based information services?

A. FIND/SVP, Washington Researchers, Environment Information Center, TCR Service, World Wide Information Services.

Q. What are their primary services?

A. Information-on-demand, document delivery, on-line searching, extended research, consulting, and publishing.

Q. Who are their primary clients?

A. Large corporations.

Q. What are the primary services offered by medium-sized firms?

A. Document delivery, research, consulting, information-on-demand, and conducting seminars.
Q. Who are their clients?
A. Mainly large corporations.
Q. What are the main services offered by small firms?
A. Manual searching, on-line searching, bibliographies, information-on-demand.
Q. Who are their clients?
A. Mainly small businesses, although large corporations and government agencies may use these firms as well.
Q. What are the main services offered by nonprofit firms?
A. On-line searching and preparation of bibliographies.

3

MARKETING

Regular efforts in the areas of publicity and selling are integral to the operation of a successful fee-based information service. The authors' survey, however, points up the fact that several individuals and/or companies use inadequate techniques to market their services or products. One head of a small fee-based information service had to start all over again after "wrongly assuming" a market. Apparently, several government agencies were offering the same information service free, which set back this particular broker's operation by eight months.

Problems of this type need not occur if the information entrepreneur develops a business plan and carefully assesses the market for his or her service or product. The Small Business Administration (SBA) reports that hundreds of thousands of small businesses fail due to inadequate planning and record keeping. Four of the services responding to the survey had taken advantage of SBA programs for entrepreneurs or SBA loans. Two that received SBA aid have become major companies in the field—Warner-Eddison Associates and Documentation Associates. SBA holds free bimonthly "prebusiness workshops" to assist entrepreneurs. Seminars, counseling, legal advice, and programs for women on how to start a small business are available free or at low cost. The Service Corps of Retired Executives (SCORE) shares business experience and knowledge with prospective business owners at no charge. These programs are available in nearly all the major cities in the United States, and meetings of regional associations (for example, SBA of New England) are open to interested parties.

Marketing and new product development are the major pitfalls for most of the fee-based information services in the survey. It is essential that these services first identify potential clients or the market before developing a product or service. By determining the needs and demands of information clientele, the information services are assessing the market and can, therefore, sell accordingly. Market research is usually overlooked by many small businesses, yet larger companies devote entire departments and programs to it. The important functions of marketing include:

1. Market research (assessment and analysis of marketplace).
2. Packaging of the product/service (designing).
3. Promotion (advertising).

In the packaging stage, the product is further developed and graphic designs (logos and such) are used to enhance the product. Careful planning and budgeting are necessary for all the marketing stages, but especially the promotional program. Advertising campaigns must be developed if the business is to have public visibility. Promotional programs are subject to available finances and resources and they vary with each business.

TECHNIQUES AND TOOLS

There are several marketing techniques and tools employed by fee-based information services; Table 5 illustrates the variety.

One of the keys to a successful promotion campaign is the creation of a name and a logo. Establishing an industry image is crucial for the visibility of a service company. Of the 105 fee-based information services included in this study, more than 40 have the word "information" or a variation (for example "info," "inform") in the business name, and 15 services begin with the word "information."

Examples of logos from fee-based information services are shown on the following pages. Although the larger and medium-sized companies are able to allocate substantial sums of money toward promotional efforts, there are a significant number of small companies and free-lancers that produce high-quality, graphically innovative brochures as well.

TABLE 5   MARKETING TOOLS EMPLOYED BY FEE-BASED INFORMATION SERVICES

Technique	Large	Medium	Small	Free-lance	Non-profit	Canadian	Internal Services	Total
Telephone Listings	4	11	10	11	5	3	—	44
Yellow Pages Adv.	2	9	7	2	1	—	—	21
Radio Ads	1	1	—	1	—	—	—	3
Television Ads	—	—	—	—	—	—	1	0
Ads in Journals	2	8	8	7	3	3	1	32
Newspaper Ads	1	5	6	7	1	2	—	22
Direct Mail/Information Brochures	5	14	18	18	17	3	2	77
Word-of-Mouth	5	17	18	31	17	7	3	98
Conferences, Meetings	4	10	15	18	12	4	1	64
Publications (Directory Listings)	3	5	4	10	10	2	—	34
Products	2	4	4	3	4	—	2	19
Seminars, Lectures	4	9	5	14	8	3	—	43
Sales Calls	3	10	8	9	2	5	1	38
Press Coverage	3	4	7	7	7	4	3	35
Inducements	2	—	—	1	1	—	—	4
Other	2	—	1	1	2	—	—	6

The logos illustrated are from the large, medium-sized, and small companies and from free-lancers, and one is from the non-profit group. The logos depict:

Information flow (FIND, INFO/MOTION).

Computer searching (The Information Retriever, Library Reports & Research Service, INFO-MART, TechSearch, INFO-SEARCH).

Questions and answers (Warner-Eddison Associates, Information Specialists, Information Associates).

Global coverage (INFORMATION ON DEMAND, Washington Researchers).

Clipping service (Packaged Facts).

Other (Documentation Associates, INFORMATRON, Regional Information and Communication Exchange).

Many medium-sized companies have developed effective mottoes. Documentation Associates of Santa Monica, California, calls itself "An Information Company" and advertises "Think of us as Paid Informers." A radio advertisement for Information Specialists of Cleveland, Ohio, refers to its head as "the answer lady" and uses the motto "You can ask us anything." Editec of Chicago has used "The Electric Library" to describe its on-line search service since its founding in 1972. Several other companies advertise as "one-stop information services" (INFORMATION ON DEMAND, Information Specialists, and others). FIND/SVP has in the past issued a similar statement but is currently utilizing "Think of Us as Your Total Business Information Resource." "Rent a Librarian" and "Librarian-on-Call" are popular among the free-lancers, many of whom are degreed librarians.

Few nonprofit organizations or internal services produce attractive brochures and have developed logos. Only three of the Canadian services have brochures and of these, only one is graphically designed. The majority of promotional literature received by the authors for this book consisted of single-page or sheet flyers (with single or double folds), which had been offset-printed. There have been several market studies on the subject of sales and coloring of products and the relationship between them. Blue products were the most frequently chosen by consumers, with red and yellow following. FIND, INFO/MOTION, Information Associates, and Library Reports and Research Service all use blue in their promotional literature. INFORMATION ON DEMAND uses red, and INFO-MART and INFORMATRON use yellow.

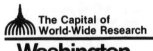

TechSearch

Information Associates Ltd.

? → info/motion™

INFO-MART
P.O. BOX 2400, SANTA BARBARA, CA 93120

Regional
Information
&Communication
Exchange

* INFORM**a**TRON

Telephone Directory Listings

Of the 105 fee-based information services surveyed, 44 have telephone listings in directories. A very small percentage take out advertisements in the Yellow Pages. Of the 21 that do, 16 are small and medium-sized companies. Yellow Pages subject headings may pose a problem for information services. The headings established for most of the major cities are Library Research Service, Library Research and Service, Market Research and Analysis, or Marketing Research and Analysis. Several information services do not choose to be listed under those headings.

In 1973, Warner-Eddison Associates of Boston had difficulty trying to establish the heading Library Research Service. They are still the only entry under that heading in the city's Yellow Pages directory, but they also have an advertisement that appears under Market Research and Analysis. The Los Angeles Yellow Pages, on the other hand, has several entries under Library Research and Service, including seven of the information services in this survey. A more appropriate heading, Information Services and Bureaus, appears only in the Manhattan Yellow Pages directory and five of the information services are listed there (FIND, Packaged Facts, Information for Business, INFORMATRON, and the World Trade Information Center). Two of these services have advertisements that appear in this section as well.

Information services that listed themselves in the Yellow Pages will often be found under two headings. For example, FIND, Information for Business, and the World Trade Information Center are also listed under Market Research and Analysis. (FIND also has an advertisement in this section.) Packaged Facts has an additional listing under Library Research Service and an advertisement under Clipping Bureaus, since its speciality is back-dated clipping services. In Chicago, Editec is the only information service listed and its entry is only under Information Bureaus. The large number of tourist boards and visitor information bureaus under this particular heading present a problem since they overwhelm the information services listings.

Infrequently, information services are listed in two different directories either within the same state or in other states. INFORMATRON , a medium-sized information service in New York City, appears in the Manhattan Yellow Pages under Information Services and Bureaus and in the Washington, D.C., Yellow Pages under both Market Research and Analysis and Information Bureaus. Information Unlimited, the predecessor of INFORMATION ON DEMAND of Berkeley, California, is listed in the Los Angeles as well as the San Francisco and Oakland directories under both Library Research and Service and Marketing Research and Analysis (only in San Francisco directory).

Radio and Television Advertising

Only three information services surveyed advertise on the radio. Of these, only one produces a regular radio spot—Information Specialists of Cleveland, Ohio. INFORMATION ON DEMAND and FIND have produced commercials and have plans for future advertisements. None of the information services has yet made television commercials.

Professional Journal Advertising

Several of the respondents indicated advertising in professional and/or trade journals as a fairly effective medium. Only 32 of the 105 services, however, take out advertisements in journals. Less than a dozen of these take out regular advertisements in library and information science periodicals, examples of which are shown in the composite illustration on the following page. The publications that carry the advertisements are *Information World, Information Manager,* and *Special Libraries.* The first two began in 1978; the third is published by the Special Libraries Association (SLA).

Newspaper Advertising

Of the 22 information services that take out newspaper advertisements, only a few can afford to place them in the large dailies. FIND and Washington Researchers have placed ads in the *New York Times* and the *Washington Post* respectively, on an irregular basis. Several small and medium-sized companies take out advertisements in local newspapers, but more than one respondent commented on the low cost-effectiveness of this technique.

Direct Mail/Information Brochures

Promotional literature is produced by 77 of the 105 information services, and it varies dramatically. These pieces include descriptions of information services and reprints of journal and/ or newspaper articles. The costs incurred from printing and

mailing range from several hundred to thousands of dollars, depending on the extent of packaging and the size of the mailing. Mailing lists are usually bought by the larger information services at costs ranging from $30–$40 per thousand names, and upward.

Although many of the respondents indicated that direct mailings were equally as effective as word-of-mouth, a few of the larger services noted that they were minimally effective unless supplemented by follow-up sales calls and/or word-of-mouth. The smaller companies and free-lancers tend to rely on their own personal contacts and send their mailings to individuals they know through former working relationships rather than to people they do not know personally, to companies, or to departments.

Word-of-Mouth

Ninety percent of all the survey respondents chose word-of-mouth as their most effective marketing technique. It is apparent that with any newly established industry, company identification on a national level is hard to achieve. The company with the most visibility in the information service industry is FIND. Its powerful advertising campaign and sales force have enabled FIND to corner most of the market in New York City. Its client listing includes an impressive array of large corporations with headquarters in New York City and along the East Coast.

Even FIND's visibility will not make fee-based information services "household words" in the near future. Business and industry will undoubtedly remain the major clientele for information services for some time, although personalized services such as genealogical research should continue to flourish among individual clients. Clients provide invaluable feedback on the quality of service, and for word-of-mouth to be generated, the information service has to establish a good reputation and high performance standards. Small businesses cannot afford to lose customers, especially if the loss is due to poor service or mismanagement. Maintaining a good rapport with all clients is of paramount importance since word-of-mouth can have the reverse effect, in the sense that bad rapport will not promote business. Independent information specialists work extremely hard encouraging word-of-mouth referrals because they usually do not have large-scale promotion campaigns as a backup. To be successful, people in this field must possess outgoing personalities and be able to communicate effectively. All of the free-lancers surveyed indicate that they obtain business through referrals. Only half utilize direct mail or attend conferences, and they use them as supplemental marketing tools.

Several respondents feel that government information services are starting to move in on their territories. Often the government services are attached to large academic institutions—for example, the National Aeronautics and Space Administration Industrial Applications Centers, the Western Research Application Center at the University of California–Los Angeles (WESRAC) and the New England Research Application Center at the University of Connecticut (NERAC)—and will price themselves competitively in the marketplace. The impact is severe for some of the fee-based information services that offer, in particular, on-line searching. Word-of-mouth keeps several fee-based information companies out in front. One pioneer on the West Coast stated: "There is room for creative and imaginative marketing and production techniques, for new services, and for companies of many kinds."[1]

Conferences, Professional Institutes, and Meetings

More than half of the survey respondents attend conferences and meetings, but only a small percentage exhibit at such functions. At the Information Industry Association's (IIA) National Information Conference and Exhibition (NICE) III, only five major information services exhibited: FIND/SVP, Environment Information Center, Washington Researchers, INFORMATION ON DEMAND, and Warner-Eddison Associates. The costs for exhibitions are significant, ranging from $500–$700 per booth depending on location. Professional contacts and the information exchanges that occur at these conferences are significant.

Directory Listings

Only the free-lancers and the nonprofit information services indicate a substantial amount of business obtained from free directory listings; 14 of the other services feel that directory listings do generate some business. Several company heads who were interviewed noted that the listings in the *Directory of Fee-Based Information Services* were of use when looking for services with which to subcontract and that the directory was a tool more for the trade than for their clients.[2] A few members of larger firms feel that the directory could also serve as an acquisitions guide for those companies who wish to acquire others. (To the authors' knowledge, few information service conglomerates are in existence and only one or two services indicated a willingness to be acquired.)

Products (newsletters, market reports)

Of the 19 information services in which staff feel that their products help to generate more business, none find them a truly effective marketing tool. Most of the products are research reports, bibliographies, directories, or guides to sources of information. Some fee-based information services publish newsletters, such as:

> *Brainstorms,* published irregularly by INFO-MART, available free, Box 2400, Santa Barbara, CA 93120.

> *CTRC Newsletter,* a quarterly (volume 10, 1980) available free from Colorado Technical Reference Center, Campus Box 184, Norlin Library, University of Colorado, Boulder, CO 80309.

> *Findout,* a bimonthly (volume 7, 1980), $20 a year, published by FIND/SVP, 500 Fifth Ave., New York, NY 10036.

> *Information Management,* available monthly (volume 1, 1980) at £24 yearly (US $60), from NPM Information Services Ltd., New Product Management, Management House, Parker St., London WC2B 5PU, England.

> *The Information Report,* a bimonthly (volume 6, 1980), available for $24 yearly from Washington Researchers, 918 16 St. NW, Washington, DC 20006.

> *The Informer,* a free quarterly (volume 4, 1980), published by Documentation Associates, 1513 Sixth St., Santa Monica, CA 90401.

> *Questnews,* irregular publication of Omniquest, Inc., Box 15, Chappaqua, NY 10514, free.

> *Umbrella,* a bimonthly from Umbrella Associates, Box 3692, Glendale, CA 91201, $12.50 a year.

> *Unlimited Access,* free, irregular publication from INFORMATION ON DEMAND, Box 4536, Berkeley, CA 97404.

Seminars, Lectures, Workshops

Conducting seminars, lectures, or workshops is economically viable for 43 information services surveyed. The free-lancers lead in this category, and only internal information services do not participate in any seminar or workshop activity. Many of the larger information services advertise their seminars—FIND has offered database seminars for business executives and has promoted them in professional and trade journals and newspapers; Washington Researchers offers 6 seminars annually (bimonthly) on various topics of interest to business personnel, researchers, information specialists, and the like, and has large mailing lists for the several promotional flyers it produces for each seminar. Several of the principals interviewed have been invited to appear on panels or to present an overview of their business operations at library school institutes or regional and state library association meetings instead of arranging for their own presentations. Thus, the high number of free-lancers participating in seminars is based on the number of appearances made rather than the number of self-sponsored presentations. Furthermore, seminars create visibility for information services and their principals.

Sales Calls

Sales calls are considered an aggressive marketing technique by those who do not make them. Those who do make regular sales calls rate the technique on the same level of effectiveness as word-of-mouth and direct mail. Of the 38 information services that make sales calls, 9 are free-lancers and 2 are nonprofit services. These two groups seem less inclined to use aggressive marketing techniques due to budget constraints and/or personal philosophies. The larger information services are able to devote more staff and time to this area of marketing than can operations with fewer than seven staff personnel. One medium-sized company offers a variation on this technique whereby it makes personal contact via letter and then follows up with a telephone interview.

Press Coverage

There is a definite pattern of press coverage for the information services surveyed. The larger companies are usually covered by national press and the smaller companies by local press. Of the 35 information services that indicated receiving editorial coverage in specialized press, fewer than 5 say it is the most effective marketing tool. Several respondents commented on the usefulness of reprints in producing their promotional packages. The far-reaching effects on the marketplace are usually limited to press coverage of the large companies. For example, FIND and Washington Researchers have been written up in the *New York Times* and the *Washington Post* respectively. These papers have greater distributions than most of the local presses combined. An information service that is highlighted in a professional journal receives some degree of recognition within that professional group or association. There are several principals of information services who are members of SLA and have also received press coverage in its journal, *Special Libraries*. Free-lancers and small information services, on the other hand, receive a significant amount of local press coverage. Reprints from local presses were sent to the authors from many small and independent information services.

Inducements

The least popular marketing tool among information services is the inducement or "gimmick." Only four services obtain business in this way. Special introductory rates are used to attract new customers. FIND offers a free minicalculator to those clients who successfully refer other businesses to the company as retainer account customers. None of the services list inducements as an effective marketing technique. The nonprofit service that offers special rates does so only for students who pay for on-line searches in advance.

Six information services have variations of the inducement technique. Two major services emphasize reputation and work excellence as their calling cards. One small-company respondent is pleased with the number of its free listings in several directories on the market, and one free-lancer feels that his public service work has very high visibility. Of the two nonprofit services that mentioned additional techniques, one produces specialized advertisements in various media and the other receives referrals from an internal department. One free-lancer writes articles for professional journals, noting that the print exposure is beneficial.

The concept of information marketing has yet to be fully developed. Educating the end user or potential client is integral to the selling of any information service and the marketing of the information industry as a whole. Information as a commodity, an economic resource, and an industry is the major concern of IIA, which promotes the concept that information can be tapped, capitalized, or expensed, explaining in its annual directory:

Information, like finance, personnel, space and materials, is a resource with costs and benefits. . . . For some companies the marketing of information is their primary, if not only, enterprise. For others, it is part internal tool and part marketable product. Almost universally, however, multiple uses of the same information—through spin-off, reformatting, segmenting, and the like—help to make it a growth industry.[3]

Efforts are underway to launch a nationwide information industry publicity campaign, which will have direct impact on all segments of the industry. Fee-based information services will gain long-range benefits from extensive public relations efforts by IIA, which provides the umbrella support necessary for raising potential user consciousness toward these services. Since its founding in 1971, IIA has been developing at about the same rate as the industry as a whole. It is an effective vehicle for lobbying for information policies and decisions on national and international levels, and fee-based information services have not yet realized its full benefits.

BASIC QUESTIONS AND ANSWERS

Q. What are some of the marketing tools used by fee-based information services?
A. Word-of-mouth, telephone listings, Yellow Pages advertising, newspaper and journal advertisements, brochures, conferences, sales calls.
Q. What do many firms consider the most effective marketing tool?
A. Word-of-mouth.
Q. What are inducements and are they effective as a marketing tool?
A. Inducements are gimmicks to attract customers (such as offering a gift to a client who brings in new business); most information firms do not consider them effective.

NOTES

1. Patricia Ferguson, "Chronicles of an Information Company," *On-Line Review* 1 (1977): 42.
2. See Chapter 1 under Study of Fee-Based Information Services for details on the directory.
3. Information Industry Association, *Information Sources 1979–80,* pp. i, ii.

4

INFORMATION-GATHERING
TECHNIQUES

Very few fee-based information services can afford to maintain extensive internal collections. Many of the larger services economize by using special library collections instead of building their own, or they subcontract with domestic or foreign information firms for specialized services that they do not offer. The respondents in this survey indicate the sources they use to answer client queries as: in-house collections, on-line databases, nearby libraries, experts contacted by telephone, other information services, and "other."

The information-gathering techniques used by these fee-based services varies according to the scope of services offered. Table 6 illustrates the number of services provided by the respondents in each category of fee-based information service. The most frequently offered services by all the respondents include consulting, research, bibliographies (compilation and/or publication), manual searching, information-on-demand, and document delivery. On-line searching, indexing, conducting seminars, selective dissemination of information (SDI), and analytical report writing are offered by more than half of the services surveyed. Other services offered by more than 30 respondents include:

Large (1): micropublications.
Medium (10): software; systems analysis and design, conversions; abstracting; card production, database develop-

TABLE 6 SERVICES OFFERED BY FEE-BASED INFORMATION SERVICES

Services	Large	Medium	Small	Free-lance	Non-profit	Canadian	Internal Services	Total
Analytical Reports	4	10	6	13	6	4	3	46
Bibliographies	3	10	19	24	16	7	3	82
Consulting	5	14	17	30	12	5	2	85
Document Delivery	5	16	15	17	13	6	3	75
Indexing	3	10	14	20	8	5	1	61
Information-on-Demand	5	12	18	17	14	6	3	75
Manual Searching	4	9	21	20	15	6	3	78
Market Reports	3	7	7	5	8	—	2	32
On-line Searching	5	9	11	17	16	5	2	65
Publications	5	5	8	11	8	3	1	41
Research (Extended)	5	15	14	28	13	6	3	84
Selective Dissemination of Information (SDI)	2	5	14	9	11	5	1	47
Seminars, Lectures	3	10	7	16	10	4	—	50
Translating	1	2	5	5	5	1	1	20
Other	1	10	7	9	4	4	1	36

ment, space planning, on-line training; information center development; records management; computerized indexing; library design, thesaurus development, clearinghouse design, information retrieval systems; micropublications; plagiarism research, arts production.

Small (7): back-dated clipping service; thesaurus development; records management; systems analysis and design; organization of library collections; software, book catalogs.

Free-Lancers (8): abstracting; picture research; editing; procedures manuals; records management; public relations and problem-solving services; architectural programming, fiscal base development; database production; communication and service orientation systems; management consulting.

Non-profit (4): out-of-print search service; multiple database searching produced on computer system; mailing lists; telephone interviewing.

Canadian (4): abstracting, editing, career counseling; computerized indexing; management consulting; editorial and writing services; book promotion, original research.

Internal Services (1): patent searching.

ANALYZING THE SOURCES

The five large firms all provide consulting, document delivery, information-on-demand, on-line searching, publications, and research services. Each has a preferred source for obtaining data to fulfill client requests—one relies on an in-house collection, another on telephoning experts, another on on-line databases. Three of the services utilize proprietary databases more than 50 percent of the time. These services are able to afford the high costs of owning several computer terminals and subscribing to more than one on-line retrieval system. One company relies primarily on telephone contacts and has extensive Wide Area Telecommunications Service (WATS) lines. Two of the companies have foreign affiliates, which they tap for statistics, unpublished data, current research, and so on.

The 17 medium-sized firms offer a wide range of services. More than half provide document delivery, research, consulting, information-on-demand, analytical reports, bibliographies, indexing, manual and on-line searching, and seminars. Nearby libraries are heavily utilized. Five firms use on-line databases more than 50 percent of the time, and only one service uses its in-house collection for 95 percent of its requests. Telephoning experts is common, but only one service uses it to obtain data as much as 80 percent of the time. Other information services are used an average of 20 percent for specialized reports, and one service, which provides East Asian research, utilizes a foreign information service 85 percent of the time. Nine others list sources such as government reference rooms (80 percent), distant libraries (20 percent), staff expertise (85 percent), published reports and research indexes (5 percent each), and various other special reports that are not readily available.

Several of the small information services also rely on nearby libraries to answer requests. More than half of the 21 small firms surveyed offer manual searching, bibliographies, information-on-demand, consulting, document delivery, indexing, research, SDI, and on-line searching. Five utilize nearby libraries for some 75 percent of their requests. On-line databases are used about half the time for 5 services; one reported this source for 95 percent of its business. Only 3 indicate using their own collections and 4 used telephone experts.

The free-lancers who responded list nearby libraries as their most frequently used source; 28 of 31 use them about half the time to answer requests. On-line retrieval services are popular with half of these services, and 4 use on-line databases for answering more than 50 percent of their queries. In-house collections, personal resources, and telephone contacts are used 5–20 percent of the time. Since most free-lancers are degreed librarians, they are usually aware of the best sources of information in their area and are able to subcontract with other information services for on-line searching or other specialized services. Informal networks exist among the free-lancers, which enable them to communicate easily and share sources of information. California independent information specialists, in particular, are aware of colleagues in the field and often engage in reciprocal agreements for services.

Canadian information services primarily provide bibliographies, document delivery, information-on-demand, manual searching, and research. None produce market studies and only one offers a translating service. Nearby libraries are used by three of the seven services more than half of the time for answering requests. Two services utilize on-line retrieval systems about 90 percent of the time, and the telephone is least used, with two reporting more than 20 percent usage.

All of the internal services rely extensively on their in-house collections to answer requests. Only one of the three indicated using on-line databases for 80 percent of its requests. The services offered by all internal services include analytical report writing, bibliographies, document delivery, information-on-demand, manual searching, and research. None of the internal services offer seminars, lectures, or workshops. These services are usually hidden within the parent companies and have limited exposure.

In-house Collections

In-house collections include reference works (directories, guides to sources of information, abstracts, and indexes), company files (annual reports, Securities and Exchange Commission reports), and periodicals/trade journals. Few of the surveyed information services have extensive, heavily used in-house collections. (FIND and Warner-Eddison Associates have sizable collections of over 5,000 items.) The nonprofit information services and internal services of large corporations rely heavily on internal collections. This is due, primarily, to the availability of the corporate library or information center. All of the internal services use in-house libraries more than 50 percent of the time. Developing and maintaining an in-house collection is very costly and time consuming. Many information services have collections of trade directories and/or telephone books, which they refer to as their library.

On-Line Databases

The market for on-line services has been increasing since the mid-1970s, and its impact on the information industry is apparent in the number of individuals providing this service for a fee. In early 1980, a leading on-line retrieval vendor estimated more than 200 individual subscribers to its system. (The number of U.S. company subscriptions is estimated at 225). This figure includes end users other than librarians or information brokers. There is no separate tracking system for ascertaining the actual number of fee-based information firms that subscribe to on-line retrieval services.

Sixty-five respondents to this survey provide on-line search services. The free-lancers and nonprofit services lead in this category. One California information specialist has produced his own software package for conducting customized searching for clients, called the Information Broker's Automated Terminal System, which is described in a brochure for prospective clients. Parts of promotional literature from other firms are shown in the following pages.

The costs of establishing an on-line search service are high. Each system also offers periodic training and refresher courses, which are essential for those involved with daily search requests. Several information firms subscribe to more than one on-line retrieval service. A few specialize in subject areas and subscribe to the legal services, LEXIS or WESTLAW, or to medical services, MEDLINE or MEDLARS.

On-line search services are still popular among the smaller information firms, but the growing marketplace in big business will affect the role of the information specialist. In the past the information specialist produced the search package for the client, but the future role will be expanded to include analytical and evaluative functions. Software packages for on-line retrieval are becoming suitable for use by nonlibrarians, and computer terminals will probably be fully adopted in the marketing and industrial sectors by the 1990s.

Nearby Libraries

Nearby libraries were the most frequently cited source for obtaining data for research, document delivery, information-on-demand, and consulting services offered by the fee-based information services that were surveyed. Only the five larger companies and the internal services indicate low percentages of external library usage. Since several of the information services and/or their employees belong to the library associations, reciprocal borrowing privileges are granted through the memberships. Over half of the survey respondents belong to the Special Libraries Association (SLA), and this membership gives them access to corporate, legal, financial, medical, and other libraries or information centers. One California information service has limited borrowing privileges at a major university located within walking distance. Document-delivery services are provided by 75 of the respondents who reported heavy utilization of libraries. Interlibrary loan (ILL) requests and/or field staff are needed to gather photocopies of requested materials, and reciprocal arrangements with special libraries allow fast and reliable processing.

User chargers are sometimes levied by libraries, but this has

INFORMATION ORGANIZING

Custom Data Summaries
Written reports can be tailored to your
specifications summarizing data collected
through our services.

Thorough Indexing Services
INFORMATION on DEMAND indexes
literature, technical reports or company data
using IODex™, our own proprietary software.
Clients receive indexes arranged by subject
in Key-Word-In-Context (KWIC) format, by
author and source and a complete bibliography of their collections. Traditional subject
indexing and hierarchical thesaurus building
are also available.

Internal Information Management
INFORMATION on DEMAND will evaluate
your information resources and requirements
and make recommendations or implement
needed changes. **IOD** can also establish or
reorganize an in-house library or information
center.

Expert Translations
Materials are translated into the target
language by translators with advanced
degrees in engineering and the sciences.
We specialize in foreign patents and maintain
the lowest rates possible, consistent with producing high quality, edited translations.

Custom Services
We design custom services to meet your
unique information demands.

ON-LINE SEARCHING

What is on-line literature searching?

It is an information gathering technique that can directly retrieve, using a computer terminal, relevant citations to current literature on topics of interest in such fields as engineering, business, social science, physics; electronics, computer science, management, the environment, agriculture, chemistry, forest products, energy, pulp and paper, food, geology, marketing, biology, and many others. Sources of the literature may include journals, patents, trade magazines, technical reports, conference proceedings, theses, books, and government documents.

What do you get?

A computer-produced bibliography customized to the subject you specify. For quick results, citations can be displayed in various formats right at the terminal. If you prefer, search results can be printed off-line on 8½ x 11 paper, suitable for filing. (An off-line printout will reach you generally about one week after the search has been run.) Each citation, whether on-line or off-line, contains a full reference to the printed document (author, title, publication source, date, etc.) Many of the data bases supply an abstract as well. Since the computer terminal used is a handy portable model, the on-line search can be conducted in your office, if you wish.

not been a deterrent since many information services pay annual fees to academic or corporate libraries.

Telephoning Experts

The larger and medium-sized information services utilize this method more than do the smaller, nonprofit, free-lance, or internal services. Washington Researchers relies exclusively on telephone contacts with government employees for its research and information-on-demand services. Free-lancers usually cannot afford the long-distance tolls; however, they phone personal contacts (such as librarians in special libraries) and rely on free referral services. Telephoning enables the information service to gain current data on any topic where there might be ongoing research or unpublished material. This technique supplements manual and on-line searching and is an effective means of gathering necessary data. Several firms indicate that they serve as a neutral third party in obtaining information in this manner and that the confidentiality of the client is always assured.

Other Information Services

Subcontracting and reciprocal agreements with other information services are popular among the larger companies. Through special arrangements with foreign firms, FIND, Documentation Associates, INFORMATION ON DEMAND, and Information Specialists, to name a few, have access to specialized information that is difficult to obtain in the United States. These companies utilize foreign services to obtain data for 10 percent of their requests. Several free-lancers subcontract with larger information firms for on-line search services in particular. Percentages for utilization of other services by free-lancers ranges from 1 to 5.

BASIC QUESTIONS AND ANSWERS

Q. What are the main sources used by information services to gather data?

A. In-house collections, on-line databases, nearby libraries, experts contacted by telephone.

Q. What do in-house collections contain?

A. Reference works (directories, guides to information sources, abstracts, and indexes), company files, and periodicals/trade journals.

Q. Why do many of these firms belong to the Special Libraries
   Association?
A. Membership gives them access to corporate, legal, financial,
   medical, and other libraries or information centers.
Q. Can fee-based information services obtain data outside of the
   United States?
A. Yes, some U.S. companies have special arrangements with
   foreign firms to obtain information that is hard to locate in
   this country.

5

ECONOMICS OF THE INDUSTRY

Few industries begin with as little capitalization as fee-based information services. More than half of those responding to the survey started with an initial investment of less than $1,000. Typical is the California organization, now in the top 10 percent in size, that began with $250 for business cards and stationery.

Given such low capitalization, most information services undertake short projects for which they can be paid on completion or shortly thereafter. For all but the large firms, invoices range from $75 to $200. Less than 10 percent of the information services regularly prepare invoices for $2,000 or more.

Cash-flow problems seem a chronic condition of the majority of the services. No one characterized his or her company as highly profitable, and payrolls were often hard to meet, particularly in the first three years. Most heads of information services had little prior experience as top managers, which may account for the fact that many information services fail or are marginally profitable. However, the failure rate for these firms is lower than for small businesses generally, 80 percent of which fail in the first three years.

Information services have three forms of business organizations—sole proprietorship (the largest number), partnership, and corporation. In the sole proprietorship, one person owns the business, although he or she may employ a number of others. Income is reported on the individual's tax return.

Although several fee-based partnerships have been established, the majority subsequently became sole proprietorships or corporations. Partnership income is not taxed. It flows through the partnership to the individual partners, who pick up their distributive shares. Partnership agreements are often informal at first, but they must be more clearly defined as the business grows to fix salaries and duties, allocate losses, and such. One partner is responsible for the actions of the others, and each is personally liable for any losses or suits brought against the business.

A corporation is generally a separate taxable entity under which shareholders report all income on their personal returns. A corporation usually costs about $1,000 to set up. Annual tax returns are more complex than personal returns, costing approximately $250 to have prepared. The tax rate, if there is income, is 18–20 percent on income under $50,000 per year. In addition to limiting the personal liability of the shareholders to their investments, the corporation can deduct many expenses, such as "key man" life insurance, medical coverage for the whole family, and contributions to pension and profit-sharing plans.

The majority of those who selected the corporate form of organization retain accounting services at a cost of $75 or more per month. Many of those who chose other forms of organization do their own bookkeeping.

For most information services, staff costs are the largest single factor, so prices are normally based on the level and amount of staff time necessary to do the work. Simple information retrieval normally costs less than work that requires analysis. The rates charged may be as little as $15 per hour for the former and as much as $75 per hour for the latter. Very small firms often do not charge more than $35 per hour for any of their services; larger firms seldom charge less than $25 per hour for even the simplest work. Salaries for staff range from $10,000 per year or less to as much as $25,000. The higher rates of the larger information services reflect another important cost factor—overhead. The smaller services spend less on offices, marketing, employee benefits, and other categories. Also, the principal(s) in a small service may forgo regular salary checks in the first year or more of operation.

In order to base pricing on costs, an information service must have reliable cost information, not only on salaries but on every aspect of the business. Most of those interviewed do not have such cost data and tend to rely on impressions, trial and error, and checking of competitors' prices. Some costs were obtained, however, in the in-person interviews conducted by the authors.

Fringe benefits cost as little as 15 percent for those that offer only the required social security, unemployment insurance, and 15–20 days of vacation, holidays, and sick leave, to 35 percent for those that also offer medical and dental insurance, retirement, profit sharing, and educational benefits. Office costs, for those who maintain quarters outside the home, range from $10 to more than $25 per square foot per year. This translates into as much as $3,750 per year per person.

Telephone information gathering is an important technique for most information services, but only the largest can afford Wide Area Telecommunications Service (WATS) for low-cost, high-volume long distance services from AT&T. Several principals used home telephones for business initially to avoid the $250 or more deposit required for a business installation.

Office equipment costs are minor for most information services. Furniture tends to be converted from private use or purchased secondhand. The only major investment usually is photocopy equipment, rented at from $50 to more than $400 per month or purchased at $1,900 to $8,000 and up. Several information services rely on coin-operated equipment at nearby libraries or on commercial copying firms rather than making this large investment.

Marketing costs for some information services are as little as the price of a Yellow Pages listing and the printing of letterhead stationery, but a few firms retain full-time experienced marketing specialists. Some Yellow Pages advertisements cost more than $1,000 per year, and the promotional brochures used by one information service cost more than $1.50 apiece to print and distribute. A few services have purchased mailing lists at $30–$40 per thousand names and have done direct mailings costing up to $1 per addressee.

Most services have a relatively small number of clients and a high percentage of repeat business. Few services have successfully negotiated progress payments or advances on expenses. Document-delivery prices may range from $5.25 to $7.50 per article or higher, plus photocopying and royalty charges. The photocopying prices range from $.05 to $.40 per page. Another $1 might be added for mailing. A five-page article might, therefore, cost a client as much as $10. Rush service might add $2.50–$10 more.

The leader in document-delivery service, INFORMATION ON DEMAND of Berkeley, California, processes 8,000 requests per month. Most of the other firms count their volume in the hundreds of items monthly. Even a firm that uses field staff paid by the hour rather than salaried personnel to go to libraries to retrieve and photocopy materials cannot make a significant and predictable profit from this service. One of the problems is that materials may not be immediately available or copy machines may be busy or out of order, or there may be little cooperation from the library.

The most experienced information services protect themselves against the hidden costs of document-delivery services by providing highly detailed price schedules to clients itemizing many special services. Among the most common is a provision that incorrectly given citations are subject to a verification charge, which usually ranges from $4–$5.

A number of services give retainer account clients a $.50 or greater discount for this service. A few large for-profit information services have relied, in part, on nonprofit services such as the Engineering Societies Library. Each charges $1–$2 less than the for-profit organizations for photocopy services.

Free-lancers and small firms usually bill document delivery to the client on completion because they want to recover costs as quickly as possible. Most have set minimums for services, reflecting an awareness of the high overall cost of billing in the organization. One firm estimates that handling accounts receivable costs 10 percent of the entire operating budget of the organization. Those that can afford to do so bill monthly to reduce the costs of invoicing. The well-established firms seek deposit accounts and charge services against the deposit, providing periodic accounting to the client. A minimum deposit is usually $100.

The subscription or retainer basis of charging for nonresearch is particularly popular with the incorporated information services. It provides a more predictable cash flow and a basic income from which fixed costs can be paid. The retainer also has the advantage of encouraging a client to continue to use the service. The subscription or retainer is usually negotiated according to the likely level of use by the client. A tentative figure is set for the first two or three months and adjusted to reflect actual usage. The typical client spends $150–$250 per month, but some services will maintain a retainer for as little as $75 per month.

More than half of the information services do on-line searching, in most cases using their own purchased or rented terminals. A terminal suitable for the searching of the Lockheed database, for example, costs approximately $2,200. This is the largest capital cost that most of the smaller information services have. The actual costs of searching are passed on to the clients and can often be recovered by the time the service has to pay the database vendor. Database access charges may range from $25–$150 per on-line connect hour (including payment of royalties, which normally constitute one-third of the database charge). Prices for access and printing of citations off-line are variable and range from $.05–$.50 per citation. Communications costs are usually $5–$10 per Tymshare or Telenet connect hour. A typical ten-minute search of the most frequently used databases costs approximately $15.

Some information services keep a log on each project and record both estimated and actual time and costs for each to determine the profitability of the work performed. One principal in a medium-sized company regularly analyzes the logs to change rates and to adjust work assignments among his small staff, but this technique is not common practice.

Several information services have concluded that the "high-volume" services such as document delivery and on-line searching do not generate much profit. They are, therefore, constantly exploring new services that will be profitable. Custom-tailored market studies are a major potential source of income—up to $8,000 for a 200-page report for a study that may take up to two months of research and writing. An organization has to have a good cash position to commit this much time before billing the client. In fact, the salaries are usually paid out 60 to 90 days before payment is received for such projects.

Publications are a potentially profitable area. A majority of the larger information services have become publishers. Several used the term "repackaging" to describe the practice of selling information they have gathered over and over again. The lowest priced publications offered by an information service are those produced by Washington Researchers. The company's directories of various information sources, particularly governmental, are priced as low as $5. Its most expensive directory is $95. FIND/SVP, on the other hand, typically charges from $50 to $850 for published reports. Washington Researchers relies on relatively large distribution. FIND makes only a few sales of each highly specialized report.

Publications may be created from in-house files generated in the course of answering quick-information questions, performing searches, or conducting market studies, or they may be obtained from other information services that lack the capacity to market their own publications. The income from sales is then shared more or less equally between the two companies.

A high-cost area, but one that can produce excellent profits, is that of special institutes or seminars. Arrangements for a one-day program for 100 persons will cost at least $5,000 in any major city, but at $100 per registrant, the income is $10,000. The average daily fee for seminars given by information services included in this study is in excess of $125 and the maximum is $350. High-quality mailing lists are vital in effectively promoting this service. The leaders in the field purchase lists and gradually refine them.

Large in-house collections are not common in the majority of information services surveyed. No major capital outlay is normally made for materials. Initially, the services rely on nearby libraries. When in-house collections are built up, they often consist of unpublished or highly specialized items. Among the large in-house collections identified during the site visits were government documents, telephone directories, annual reports of corporations, and photocopies of journal articles previously supplied to clients.

All operating costs, including salaries to principals, add up to as much as 70–85 percent of revenues for information services established more than one year. This leaves very little for income taxes and profit. In the light of the small margins that prevail in a labor-intensive industry, one might expect many of the businesses to obtain bank or Small Business Association (SBA) loans. However, that does not appear to be the case. The majority of those interviewed chose to finance their businesses from savings rather than from loans. Most did not know of the available SBA programs. One of the 10 largest firms in the field, however, attributes its growth to a timely loan in its second year of operation. That made it possible for the firm to grow from a partnership to a corporation employing several people, allowing the principals to concentrate on marketing, development, and overall management activities. A few nonprofit information services, primarily in academic institutions, received seed capital from the National Science Foundation.

BASIC QUESTIONS AND ANSWERS

Q. How are fee-based information services organized?
A. As corporations, partnerships, or sole proprietorships.
Q. What is the most common form of organization?

A. Sole proprietorship.

Q. How does the failure rate for information firms compare with the rate of failure for small businesses in general?

A. The failure rate for small businesses in general is much higher; 80 percent fail in the first three years.

Q. What is the largest cost factor for the information firm?

A. Staff expenses.

Q. What rates do fee-based companies charge?

A. Rates can vary from $15 per hour for simple information retrieval to $75 per hour for work that requires analysis.

6

FIND/SVP—A Close-Up

Eleven stories above Fifth Avenue in midtown New York City are the offices of FIND/SVP, The Information Clearinghouse. FIND is one of several independent companies affiliated with the French research firm SVP (S'il Vous Plait), headquartered in Paris. In addition to FIND, there are affiliates in Toronto (SVP Canada), Tokyo (Nikkei SVP Co., Ltd./Japan), Milan (SVP Italia), Brussels (SVP Benelux), Basel (SVP Conseil, originally in Geneva), Mexico City (SVP Mexico), Sydney (SVP Australia), Johannesburg (SVP South Africa), Seoul (SVP Korea), and SVP correspondents in Great Britain, Germany, Spain, Denmark, Sweden, Argentina, Brazil, and more recently in the Philippines, Thailand, and the Middle East. Members of the confederate meet annually in one of the designated SVP cities.

Worldwide, there are more than 20,000 subscribers to SVP, the oldest fee-based information service. It is the only firm in the industry to have an extensive global network and a multimillion dollar revenue. The Paris operation (SVP France), which was founded in the 1940s, has more than 12,000 subscribers. A staff of 300 researchers processes 4,000 plus queries daily from domestic and foreign firms in France. In comparison, the New York operation has more than 600 subscribers and its staff of about 50 receives 3,000 to 3,500 inquiries monthly from the United States and from U.S.–based foreign companies. Thus, FIND is among the largest fee-based information services in the country—annual revenues exceed $3 million.

Incorporated in 1969, FIND leads the industry with its unique approach to information retrieval and contract research services. FIND describes itself as a "total business information resource" dedicated to providing complete-in-one-house access to a line of information products and services.

One of FIND's major sections, the Quick Information Service (QIS), received the Information Industry Association's (IIA) Product of the Year Award in 1974. Staffed by 30 professionals (70 percent with training in library and information science), QIS functions as a data center providing quick reference and information-gathering services. Most requests require less than two hours of research time and are processed within two working days; 90 percent of the requests are via telephone. Customers for this service are retainer-account or deposit-account clients who pay between $80 and $1,500 per month ($180 is the average). "Information cards" are issued to these clients, enabling them to dial directly into the service department that handles their account. With one phone call, clients can tap the large in-house collection consisting of 10,000 subject files, 8,000 company files (annual, SEC), government documents, some 600 trade journals, and various business reference works. Furthermore, over 200 databases, including the *New York Times* Information Bank and the Dow Jones News Retrieval Service, can be searched on one of FIND's several computer terminals. The worldwide SVP network further enhances FIND's resources, and a team of field investigators has access to an additional 200 libraries in the New York City and Washington, D.C., areas.

FIND's Document Retrieval Service is priced competitively with other fee-based information firms. This service is included within the retainer account but also offered separately on a one-time basis. It is an integral part of QIS. The fixed fee of $6 allows for up to 10 photocopied pages plus royalty charges. Non-deposit- or nonretainer-account clients are charged an additional $.50. Mail and telex requests for document retrieval account for 5 and 4 percent respectively of the total number of requests received. Phone or rush services are also available.

The Research Projects Service functions as a comprehensive custom research department, specializing in analytical reports, market surveys and studies, industry overviews, consulting and data gathering, corporate planning assistance, and acquisition analyses; 85 percent of the clients are engaged in marketing, planning, and research activities. Research fees vary and clients are billed separately from their retainer accounts. Requests from nonretainer clients are also serviced.

Additional specialized services include the Current Awareness Service, which monitors specific companies, industries, products, or trends; the Wall Street Research Report Clearinghouse, a special arrangement with Wall Street investment firms and analysts for the distribution and marketing of reports; a Direct Mail List Service; and Healthcare and Food Information Centers, which provide topical research and published studies. Clients range from top management and finance departments to advertising and public affairs personnel.

The Information Products Division publishes newsletters, directories, and market and industry reports. FIND's retainer clientele is entitled to discount rates of 5–10 percent and receives two publications free of charge. *Findout*^R, "The Newsletter for People Who Use Information," is a bimonthly publication that highlights information industry news, trends, ideas, and the like. *Management Contents*^R, produced by Management Contents, Inc., of Skokie, Illinois, is a biweekly containing tables of contents of more than 200 American and foreign business journals. It is distributed by special arrangement, and photocopies of articles from business journals are available through FIND's Document Retrieval Service. *Findout* and *Management Contents* are offered to nonretainer or outside subscribers for $20 per year and $62 per year respectively.

Reciprocal arrangements with various other research firms and information services such as Packaged Facts, Predicasts, and the Environment Information Center (EIC) enable FIND to market an array of information products. In conjunction with its special network of consultants in the areas of health care, retailing, chemicals, economics, and consumer and industrial marketing research, FIND also produces its own business information reports and multiclient studies. Two of the most popular publications are *The U.S. Bottled Water Market* and *Business Opportunities in China for Pharmaceuticals, Chemicals and Hospital Supplies*. These studies reflect industry trends and retail at $650 and $2,500 respectively. Numerous other reports from FIND range in price from $50 to $2,500.

Two widely distributed products are *Findex*™ and *The Information Catalog*.™ *Findex* is an annual directory that lists some 4,000 commercially available published reports from more than 200 American and foreign market research and investment companies as well as Wall Street brokerage firms. A midyear supplement updates this reference tool, which is intended for marketing and planning executives, advertising agencies, importers/

exporters, libraries, and researchers. A quarterly publication, *The Information Catalog* has a worldwide distribution of 50,000. It contains listings of reports, studies, surveys, business and marketing reference aids (directories, guides, and the like), and items generally unavailable through direct channels. There are two sections of the catalog: "Industry, Market, and Company Studies," which incorporates "Research from Wall Street," and "Management Information Products and Services." *Computer Bank Book,* a guide to computer database search services, is also published by FIND and directed to executive clientele.

FIND's advertising campaign is extensive, including newspaper advertisements in the *New York Times* and *Wall Street Journal,* advertisements in professional and trade journals (see illustrations in this chapter). A blue logo is used on all of FIND's promotional literature and forms. The brochures have graphically innovative design features. Inducements are used to encourage client referrals, and free minicalculators are awarded to those companies that spread the word successfully. Sales calls are made to solicit and follow up inquiries produced by client referrals or advertising efforts. Specific departments and programs at FIND (Client Relations and Business Development) are assigned to this task. FIND has also held major databank seminars for management executives. Cosponsored by Dow Jones/ Retrieval, The Information Bank, Interactive Data Corporation, and Lockheed Information Systems, these seminars acquaint executives with all aspects of on-line information retrieval.

FIND's success can be attributed to several factors—effective leadership, a highly trained staff, extensive internal resources, aggressive marketing, substantial capital outlays, careful pricing strategy, and international resources. The founders are Andrew P. Garvin, president, a former journalist for *Newsweek;* and Kathleen S. Bingham, executive vice president, a former free-lance researcher.

FIND has increased 10 times in size of staff and office space since its beginnings. Over 6,000 business executives use FIND to supply needed information quickly, accurately, and at moderate cost. Clients from major consumer goods and industrial products companies, service organizations, and American-based foreign companies contact FIND, which serves as a neutral third party, to get facts. Now one of the best-known businesses in the information industry, FIND has become a recognized name in business circles, and the concept of an information clearinghouse has been fully implemented.

YOUR FIND/SVP RETAINER BUYS A $1 MILLION FACILITY

The monthly retainer fee your organization pays to FIND covers the time spent researching your questions. But is also brings you a lot more. Here's a partial list:

- Access to the resources of FIND'S comprehensive business information center, which by itself would annually cost you a six figure sum. Through FIND, for example, you subscribe to more than 600 periodicals.

- A staff of 30 expert researchers with many subject specialties on call anytime.

- Link-ups to more than 100 data banks ranging from the New York Times Information Bank to the Dow Jones News/Retrieval Service. FIND can search them for you so you save the expense of terminals and training.

- A library of 10,000 subject files, 10,000 company files, and thousands of reference works (including phone books for all major cities) all accessible with one phone call.

- A free subscription worth $40 (sent to your liaison with FIND) to MANAGEMENT CONTENTS, a publication that reprints the tables of contents of leading business journals. So you keep current on what's happening.

- A free subscription to FINDOUT, a newsletter full of ideas and tips for people who need and use information.

- Discounts on Wall Street research reports and a wide variety of other market studies and reports.

- Priority service and rates from FIND'S Research Projects Department for in-depth assignments, studies and surveys.

- Access to document retrieval services, and the ability to use FIND to obtain product samples, catalogues, annual reports - - - even theater tickets.

- The exclusive ability to access the information centers of SVP affiliates around the world. So finding out about frozen pizza sales in Australia is no problem.

- Access to FIND'S current awareness and tracking services. So you can keep an eye on your competition or a developing trend.

- The ability to anonymously gather information by telephone. Through FIND, you can plug into experts on all subjects all over the country.

- Access to special sources like Target Group Index.

- Use of FIND'S field research team to obtain information from the more than 200 public and private libraries in New York --- and from government agencies in Washington.

- A team of managers to consult with on any information problem, and experts to help you organize your library.

- In sum, a total information resource.

Find/SVP

The Information Clearinghouse
500 Fifth Avenue, New York, N.Y. 10036

7

PROFILES OF MAJOR FEE-BASED INFORMATION SERVICES

WASHINGTON RESEARCHERS—A LARGE FIRM

Founded in 1975, Washington Researchers is a leading information service with more than 500 clients and annual revenues of more than $1.5 million. Washington Researchers specializes in tapping the world's largest concentration of expertise and documentation—Washington, D.C.

The company is best known for its seminars and publications. The "flagship" conference is the Washington Information Seminar, a one-day training session offered regularly since 1976.[1] The Company Information Seminar was introduced in 1979. These seminars (also on tape) are offered in the Washington, D.C. area, and are conducted by the firm's cofounders, Matthew Lesko, chairman of the board, and Leila Knight, president. Seminar prices average $200, with special discounts available. They provide training in research techniques, strategies, and tips, and also supply supplemental resource publications. Included in the price of the Washington Seminar are: *A Researcher's Guide to Washington, D.C.*, and *The Washington Information Workbook*. The Company Seminar includes *How to Find Information about Companies* and *Company Information Case Study Book*.

Other research publications are compiled and updated annually by Washington Researchers, including *Sources of Informa-*

tion for U.S. Exporters, Industry Analysts in the Federal Government, Government Market Studies: Reports Produced by the Federal Government, Sources of State Information on Corporations, and *Country Experts in the Federal Government.* Prices range from $5 to $95. The company issues a bimonthly newsletter, *The Information Report,* "for decision-makers who know that wisdom and influence are derived from knowing where to find information" (the newsletter's subtitle). The newsletter has lists of free or inexpensive publications, services, and documents, government and private.

In addition to publications and seminar activities, Washington Researchers provides contract research, information on demand, and document retrieval services. Research projects include market studies, competitor analyses on companies, compiling of specialized market lists, and monitoring of legislation.

More than 80 percent of the clients are large corporations, Fortune 500 companies, and agencies that service major corporations. The clientele is national and international, but does not come from Washington, D.C. Clients are mainly in marketing, research and development, and corporate planning. Washington Researchers charges a flat fee of $50 per hour. The majority of the projects handled are for $500 and up.

The staff of 20 "infomaniacs" are skilled in extracting information from government and private sources and locating publications and unpublished reports. The firm does not hire librarians as researchers; in fact, the staff includes a former French pastry chef, a retired C.I.A. agent, an ex-seminarian, and several journalists. The two principals hold M.B.A.'s and belong to marketing and management, as well as library, associations. Both believe that research answers are not usually found in printed sources—not in books or computers. Instead, they look for personable people who can deal with several different research topics daily. The telephone is the key information-gathering source and the company's most valuable technique. The federal government is regarded as its in-house library.

Press coverage of Washington Researchers is widespread, in newspapers, business journals and flight publications. The company's success is attributed to its high-powered principals who are experts at tapping Washington's gold mine of information. They have expanded their operation and adapted their methods to move with the information explosion.

Washington Researchers presents: A 1-Day Seminar

on How to Find Information in Washington:

Washington, D.C. March 13, 1979

An intensive full day seminar conducted by
Matthew Lesko, President of Washington Researchers . . .

Includes two valuable
Washington Researchers publications
(See details inside)

WARNER-EDDISON ASSOCIATES—A MEDIUM-SIZED SERVICE

One of the best known among the medium-sized information services is Warner-Edison Associates, Inc., of Cambridge, Massachusetts. Since its founding in 1973, the firm has been a model for many others entering the field because its principals have been active in the Information Industry Association (IIA), Special Libraries Association (SLA), American Society for Information Science (ASIS), and as speakers at library schools and other gatherings of prospective information specialists.

Warner-Eddison has grown large enough—a full-time staff of more than 20—to be divided into three operating units: Technical Searching, Information Management, and Information Consulting. Large corporations are the principal clients (54 percent); government agencies make up 40 percent; small business 3 percent. Although the firm continues to provide all of the services it first offered (rates are $30–$50 per hour plus database and photocopying charges), it also emphasizes library design and development, personnel planning and job descriptions, space planning, indexing, vocabulary building for subject authority control, collection development, and materials purchasing.

The company markets the data management system it developed and used in setting up some of its clients' libraries. Known as INMAGIC™, the software package may be used to capture library-related bibliographic records of any type for the development of a searchable in-house database or for the printing of library cards in any one of several formats. INMAGIC can also be used to print book catalogs or prepare tapes for the production of Computer Output Microform (COM) catalogs (see front page of INMAGIC brochure).

For those clients that do not have access to a computer, Warner-Eddison offers a cataloging service. The client prepares a data entry form and sends it for entry into the firm's computer. Catalog card sets, labels, or book catalogs, and the like are prepared and sent to the client.

Warner-Eddison has an attractive array of brochures for distribution. Although word-of-mouth is regarded as valuable promotion, direct mailings and sales calls are effective as well.

Consulting has emerged as an important service for this company (rates are up to $50 per hour). One consulting assignment was for a federal agency, which involved a study of information needs and resources of the agency. WEA frequently consults

INMAGIC™

Introduction

INMAGIC™ is a data management system developed for and used by Warner-Eddison Associates, Inc. (WEA), information management and library development firm of Cambridge, Massachusetts, U.S.A.

The INMAGIC™ system is now available for in-house use by WEA customers and clients.

General

INMAGIC™ information management system is designed for minicomputers.

The user is led step by step in presentation of data definition, and in explanation of methodology and techniques. INMAGIC™ offers more "handholding" than do many Data Base Management Systems (DBMS).

Advantages of INMAGIC™ include:
- user-defined data structures
- user-defined output formats
- efficient use of storage space
- variable record length
- on-line searching capability

Automatic editing and audit features allow users to control each database created for INMAGIC™ with little or no assistance from Warner-Eddison.

Fields and Sort Capability

The system offers many fields, which are user-defined. There is no limit to field length.

Sorting may be accomplished in any manner required, and specified, by the user. INMAGIC™ currently sorts: letter-by-letter (not word-by-word); left to right; with leading articles removed; in numerical sequence; and in alphanumeric sequence. Users may easily add other sort sequences.

with companies establishing new divisional or departmental libraries and provides services for designing, implementing, and maintaining information centers.

INFORMATION ON DEMAND—A MEDIUM-SIZED BUSINESS

INFORMATION ON DEMAND is a full service information-gathering company based in Berkeley, California. Sue Rugge, president and founder, began her "information retailing" career in 1971 when she cofounded Information Unlimited, a fee-based pioneer (for more information, see Bibliography), with Georgia Finnigan. In 1978 this partnership dissolved and two new services were formed. INFORMATION ON DEMAND was founded in January 1979 with most of the Information Unlimited employees, and The Information Store was started by Finnigan across the Bay in San Francisco.

INFORMATION ON DEMAND is currently the largest full-service document delivery company in the United States, with annual sales of more than $750,000. Other services include literature searching, market research, indexing with IODex™ (Key Word in Context) system, current awareness (AWARE™), translations, information management, and consultation. However, more than 70 percent of IOD's business is with document delivery.

IOD receives more than 8,000 document retrieval requests each month. The staff of 19 at Berkeley and 15 "doc runners," or field staff, cover major libraries throughout the country, including the University of California (Berkeley, Los Angeles, and Davis), Stanford University, the Library of Congress, the National Library of Medicine, the National Agricultural Library, the John Crerar Library (Illinois Institute of Technology), the Linda Hall Library (Kansas City, Mo.), San Francisco Public Library, Countway Medical Library (Harvard University), Cornell University Library, and the Engineering Societies Library (New York City).

Prices for document retrieval start at $5.25 plus $.15 per page. More than 75 percent of the requests handled at IOD are retrieved at this price. The more obscure and esoteric requests (such as documents obtained from non-IOD staffed sources at foreign libraries or government agencies) cost $7.50 plus additional costs incurred in retrieval. Rush service costs $5 extra per item and insures 24-hour service from any IOD-staffed sources. (These prices are quoted from an IOD 1980 brochure.)

Normal turnaround time for document delivery is 72 hours for items retrieved from college libraries, 7–10 days from eastern libraries. INFORMATION ON DEMAND also maintains reciprocal agreements with foreign libraries, such as the British Library Lending Division (BLLD), and the Lenin State Library in the U.S.S.R. Turnaround time for documents from Russia usually is 3–4 weeks. Status reports are provided to requestors informing them of sources checked and any difficulties that arise during retrieval. A recent analysis of requests handled by IOD indicates over 80 percent for science and technical materials; 50–60 percent of requests for items less than two years old; 25 percent for items less than five years old; and 15 percent for those over five years old. (These statistics were provided by the director of document delivery systems for IOD.)

INFORMATION ON DEMAND provides several unique features and caters to the custom needs of its clients. One major advantage of its document delivery service is that requests are accepted in any form that is convenient to the client. No verification of source location or special forms are required, unlike other information retrieval companies. Requestors can also state the price limit for procurement of items. IOD pays a fee to the Copyright Clearing Center (CCC) and royalties are charged back to customers when applicable. Copyright charges average $1 per article for those journals registered by the CCC. Billings are on a monthly basis, mostly customized. Deposit accounts are not required for ordering documents, but IOD offers a five percent discount to those who maintain a balance equal to their average monthly billing or request 100 or more documents per month.

IOD publishes a newsletter (*Unlimited Access*) on an irregular basis (see Appendix 2). Other publications include a Bibliographic Verification Chart (developed in cooperation with Lockheed's DIALOG service) and a Union List of Specifications and Standards (jointly with CLASS, the California Library Authority for Systems and Services).

This firm was the first supplier on the DIALORDER system, which enables users to communicate directly with document suppliers (for more information, see Chapter 11). Moreover, IOD is currently the only full service document delivery company available via all three existing systems—DIALORDER, SDC's Electronic Maildrop, and TCA's (Telecomputing Corporation of America) The Source. Clients from 18 non-U.S. countries have been attracted to IOD document delivery services, and requests are handled faster through these electronic mail systems than through regular mail.

An automated tracking and billing system was installed at IOD in July 1980. The system allows IOD to keep costs down by electronically transmitting requests to doc runners at eastern libraries, thus reducing turnaround time for deliveries. The goal is to make the service as fast and efficient as possible while tailoring it to client needs. Due to the founder's past experience as a special librarian, she is particularly sensitive to the needs and demands of clients, which include corporation libraries and information centers, Fortune 500 and INC 100 companies, as well as individuals (consultants, attorneys, and others). IOD exhibits at major library and information association conferences and advertises regularly in library press and trade journals. An active member of the Information Industry Association, Rugge has consistently promoted the information service sector of the industry throughout the years.

PACKAGED FACTS—A SMALL SERVICE

Small fee-based services, with fewer than five full-time employees, often have very large accounts requiring highly specialized services. One such small firm is Packaged Facts of New York City. Most of its clients are in marketing and advertising and seek custom market reports, back-dated clippings, or advertising tear-sheets. The firm not only provides information but also analyzes and interprets it.

Packaged Facts was started in 1962 by a former marketing executive. Initially, the company offered back-dated clipping research to help clients measure the impact of a product announcement or monitor the activities of a competitor. The service complemented the numerous current clipping services with one that emphasized historical research as far back as 50 years. Even today, operating in a much broader range, the firm is still listed in the Yellow Pages under the heading Clipping Bureaus, with its ad stating Back-Dated Clippings. The "clippings" are usually photocopies of articles from the hundreds of journals arranged in boxes and on shelves throughout the company's Madison Avenue offices.

Clipping was supplemented by a tear-sheet service for advertisements. Packaged Facts will locate and provide copies of all advertisements of a product or service by systematically surveying newspapers and magazines. Most of these services are performed for $100–$300. The company normally does not take on smaller assignments except from regular customers. The high volume of work, especially the tear-sheet service, is very labor intensive.

The company's most profitable activity is its market studies, which may cost a client up to $5,000 and run 200 or more pages. The studies rely primarily on published information, although some telephone interviewing is necessary to round out the data. An example of such a study was described in a *Marketing News* feature story in 1976 (reprinted below). The study, for a large toiletries firm, considered the introduction of a full line of cosmetics. Packaged Facts prepared information on several product categories with data on market size, growth factors, competitive situations, leading brands, new product trends, advertising, promotion, and consumer usage.

Packaged Facts tells more than marketers want to know, whether it's blondes, cigars, irons, etc.

LIZ TAYLOR and some of her fans may be shocked to know that Cleopatra really was a blonde. She was not Egyptian, but Greek.

These Believe-it-or-not-type facts were among 35 pages on the story of blondes resulting from research for the original Clairol "Blondes Have More Fun" campaign several years ago. The research put Packaged Facts, New York, "on the map," according to David A. Weiss, founder and president.

Weiss, who got his marketing experience as an executive with Hicks & Greist Advertising, New York, before founding his own information service in 1962, has little trouble making cocktail party conversation ... Speaking of cocktails, did you know 1776 was not only the year of the birth of the United States but also was the year of the birth of the cocktail, supposedly invented by Betsy Flanagan, a New York State barmaid?

Well, that's one of several thousand colorful historical facts Weiss has dug up especially for the American Bicentennial ... Speaking of Bicentennials, did you know that in England, a 200th anniversary is a "bicentenary"—not a bicentennial, as in the United States?

"FORTUNATELY, THANKS to the nostalgia trend, more people are realizing the excitement and interest that can be generated by historical facts," Weiss said.

In developing historical facts for its clients, Packaged Facts directs its research to the major areas of the client's interest, relating the facts to the particular industry, product, theme, or historic personality involved.

In conjunction with such projects, the firm also researches photographs and original artwork-type materials. It can carry a project through to final form, such as a folder, pamphlet, book, or promotion piece, he said.

Packaged Facts has researched the story of terry-cloth towels for West Point-Pepperell, the story of cigars for the Cigar Institute, and the history of tickets for Ticketron. Weiss points out that the firm not only provides the information, but can analyze and interpret it and write special reports that present the material so that it can easily be acted upon.

Although it originally specialized in the research of colorful, fascinating, historical facts and anecdotes, the firm has expanded its information services until today it offers more than 50 types of specialized research for marketing, public relations, advertising, publishing, finance, law, and import-export fields.

Working on a project-by-project basis, Packaged Facts prepares many different kinds of reports for many different types of clients, but most are linked in some way to marketing. He said that market studies can be prepared from secondary data at much less cost than primary research and custom-tailored to meet marketers' needs. Such studies are the firm's most popular product.

These studies, which cost $1,000–$3,000 and usually run more than 100 pages, include research data and actual examples of everything covered—pricing sheets, print ads, TV storyboards, the market itself, manufacturers, products, distribution channels, and wholesale, retail, and consumer levels.

AN EXAMPLE OF such a study is one done for a large toiletries company considering introducing a full line of cosmetics. Packaged Facts prepared comprehensive market studies on a half-dozen product categories with data on market size, growth factors, competitive situation, leading brands, new product trends, advertising, promotion, and consumer usage.

Packaged Facts also can research a company for an ad agency that wants to try to make the company its client. Such a study would include background on the company and its competitors, their marketing approach, and their ads.

Packaged Facts will research companies that other companies may want to acquire, special markets (geriatric, Spanish-American, etc.) consumer attitudes toward, say, tomato soup, or a particular country and its people.

The firm will search for interesting historical facts for marketing and promotion campaigns. It has studied the history of electric irons and changes in infant feeding since 1776.

WHEN SOME CLIENTS found that they couldn't separate wheat from chaff in the growing quantities of data coming to them in trade publications, Weiss started a Special Monthly Monitoring Report.

This service, he said, following clients' guidelines, tracks everything published on whatever subjects interest clients. It selects whatever is important to the client, collates the data, arranges, analyzes, and interprets it, then sends the client a monthly indexed report.

The reports can cover new products, changes in brand positioning, new ad campaigns, pricing changes, new promotions, technical developments, governmental actions, patents and trademarks, and social and economic trends—all in one market.

"It's a way of coping with the information explosion," said Weiss. "It's also a handy method when you go back over the month-by-month reports to spot the trends in a particular field or market."

Packaged Facts also offers back-dated clipping research to help marketers measure the impact of an announcement, keep track of competitors' activities, or obtain background on a specific event. The service covers about 75 U.S. newspapers, 200 magazines, and nearly 1,000 trade publications and can go back sometimes as far as 50 years. He claims it's the only such back-dated clipping service in the world.

BESIDES USING public libraries, Packaged Facts had developed its own specialized information sources and its own library, which includes about 5,000 consumer and trade magazines and marketing data.

Its staff is experienced in particular subjects and all members have writing and research backgrounds. "If you know how to write, you can research better because you understand how the material will be used," said Weiss.

More marketers are finding information services valuable, he said. "Many times exactly what is needed to answer a question or solve a problem is available in published data. It just takes a specialist to find it and present it in the right framework."

The firm's clients have ranged from Air France to the San Diego Padres and from the BBC to *Playboy*. Its fact collection subjects have ranged from aardvark to Zanzibar and Weiss claims he can help whether your product is alarm clocks or safety shoes. . . . Speaking of shoes, did you know that Beau Brummell put champagne in his shoe polish for sparkle and shined the soles of his shoes as well as the uppers?

Who cares? S. C. Johnson did when it wanted the history of shoe polish researched before launching a project. . . . Speaking of launching, did you know that the custom of ship christenings derived from the bloody practice of ancient peoples sacrificing slaves when new boats were about to be launched? . . . Speaking of boats . . .

Reprint permission from *Marketing News* (Jan. 30, 1976, Vol IX, No. 14)

More than 90 percent of all orders to Packaged Facts come by telephone, but no estimates are made via phone on the first call. Packaged Facts seeks a meeting with the client or receives something in writing if the project is to be a major one, thereby helping to eliminate misunderstandings concerning client and firm requirements. Almost 85 percent of new business comes by referral from existing clients and from other information services with which Packaged Facts has close working relationships. The remainder is generated from Yellow Pages advertising. No direct mailings or other promotional techniques are used. About 30 percent of the clientele has dealt with the firm previously.

Rates are set on the basis of cost plus a predetermined profit margin. The range is $50–$75 per hour, with $60 the average fee. The firm now repackages its past studies for publication. Since it lacks the mailing lists and marketing staff to achieve a high sales volume, FIND/SVP distributes some of its publications. The company pays FIND a percentage of the sales price and receives the majority of the revenue to compensate for costs and earn a profit.

IITRI AND FRANKLIN INSTITUTE— NOT-FOR-PROFIT SERVICES

The two largest nonprofit information services are parts of major research institutes: The Computer Search Center of the Illinois Institute of Technology Research Institute (IITRI) of Chicago, and the Information Services Department of the Franklin Institute for Research in Philadelphia.

IITRI has been serving industry and government for more than 30 years and now attains more than $25 million per year in sponsored research, consulting, and fee-based information services. The information services are part of an integrated set of services that include database creation, search software development, retrospective searching, current awareness searching, and manual searching—all offered by the Computer Search Center.

The center designed CANCERLIT, a database of the National Cancer Institute. The searching software package is offered on a customer's own computer or for use on IITRI's computer. Retrospective searches are performed over a comprehensive range of more than 100 databases by a staff whose expertise includes chemistry, biochemistry, biology, physics, engineering, agriculture, and other disciplines. Current awareness searches are offered on a subscription basis for the major technical databases. Output is offered on magnetic tape, file cards, or paper. The manual search service relies on the availability of the John Crerar Library on campus, which was formerly a wholly independent scientific research library.

The Computer Search Center was established in 1969 with more than $1 million in capital. It is not the oldest of the services associated with an academic institution, but it may be the most aggressive in its marketing. The center was not established to serve the faculty, but as a link between industry and academia. The parent institution's political base in Chicago has been built on offering a wide range of services to local industry in addition to educating prospective employees of technologically oriented firms.

Although the staff numbers fewer than 10, its members have a wide range of expertise in business, technology, and the sciences. Additional services include analytical reports, bibliographies, consulting, document delivery, market reports, publications, and seminars.

Government agencies represent 60 percent of the clientele; large corporations, 20 percent; small business, 10 percent; and nonprofit agencies, 5 percent; the balance are students. Only 15 percent of the users are local. Virtually all of those served are specialists in research and development. More than 60 percent are served through an intermediary rather than directly.

IITRI uses direct mail, sales calls, publications, and conference attendance to promote its services. It finds direct mail quite successful, but benefits equally from referrals. Queries are handled half by mail and most of the rest by telephone. Fully half of the queries involve on-line database searching, but in-house collections are consulted about one-third of the time. Almost all payments for all types of services are made in advance or by subscription, an unusual pattern for extended research projects.

Like the center, each year the Franklin Institute undertakes millions of dollars of sponsored research, especially in the applied sciences, but in social and behavioral sciences as well. The institute is best known as one of the nation's finest museums of applied sciences, but its Information Services Department provides a full range of services, almost entirely to subscription clients. One-time accounts are not solicited, but they are accepted if the amount of service required is worth at least $200. Quick-information service is considered too expensive to offer.

The Information Services Department has begun to look for more substantial income sources, as have many of the larger for-profit information services. One of the most important sources of new funds is contracts for the management of information clearinghouses. Toll-free hot lines advertised on national television lead to tens-of-thousands of requests for information from the general public. Rather than charging each a small fee, the entire program is funded as part of the annual contract budget.

The Information Services Department is part of the institute's Science Information Services Organization (SISO). Related units are called the Technology Transfer Department and Toxicological Studies. These units also perform a wide range of services, including computer and manual searching, translating, and the preparation of analytical reports. All three units do more than 95 percent of their business under contract with government agencies on national and international levels. Virtually all of the clients are specialists engaged in research and development. They are contacted almost exclusively through professional meetings, seminars, and specialized publications.

Since its creation in 1961, with an appropriation of under $10,000, the staff of SISO has grown to 375 full-time members.

FACTS FOR A FEE—A PUBLIC LIBRARY SERVICE

A number of public libraries have launched programs to provide in-depth reference service for a fee. Most of them are small—fewer than five people—but they serve an unusually wide range of clients because of their strategic location in the public library. One of the earliest was Inform, the Minneapolis Public Library's unit created in 1972. Three years later, the Cleveland Public Library established Facts for a Fee to "support extensive research beyond the tax-supported free reference service." It seems typical of library-sponsored services.

The Facts for a Fee staff of three full-time people includes two professional librarians. They prepare bibliographies and undertake document delivery, indexing, information-on-demand, manual and on-line searching, extended research, and SDI services in all disciplines except the health sciences. More than half of the clients are small businesses and 20 percent are from the general public. Another 20 percent are large corporations and fewer than 10 percent are government and not-for-profit agencies. Many of the referrals come from other parts of the library, so fully two-thirds of the clients have not dealt with Facts for a Fee previously. Nearly 75 percent of all requests come from the local area and another 20 percent from the surrounding state and region.

Clients represent marketing, research and development, administration, consulting, and so on. Most (95 percent) are served directly rather than through an intermediary. Facts for a Fee uses Yellow Pages advertising, but referrals from the library staff are the most important source of new business. As an example, in 1979 there were more than 4,500 document-delivery requests and nearly 200 extended research projects. On-line databases were used 15 percent of the time and in-house collections more than 75 percent of the time to answer requests. Only 25 percent of the requests came in person and more than 50 percent by telephone. One might expect more of the referrals from regular library staff to be people who had come into the library.

The fees are $10 per hour for basic research and $25 per hour for professional research plus photocopying and on-line search costs, if any. The prices were set on the basis of analyzing the fees of commercial information services. Quick-reference questions are always answered free of charge. This information service is considered by its staff to be in competition with other (including commercial) services in the region. It measures its own performance through customer reactions and repeat business.

INTERNAL SERVICES

Some internal information organizations earn extra revenue by selling their services outside the parent companies, for example, the Arthur D. Little Information Research Section of Cambridge, Massachusetts, the Marketing Information Center of McGraw-Hill Publishing Company, New York City, and the Chase World Information Center, Chase Manhattan Bank, also in New York City. These internal services were established in the 1970s, and all are profitable within their own firms. The staffs vary in size—one has fewer than 5 people, one has 10–15, and the other has over 20. Background and experience of the principals include management, librarianship, and on-the-job training. Only one service is a member of ASIS; two belong to SLA and IIA. All three provide information-on-demand, document delivery, research, manual searching, bibliographies, and analytical reports. Only two offer on-line search services and market studies. One publishes a monthly abstracting service and one provides patent searches.

These services receive 75–95 percent of their business from the parent companies. One reports 30 percent of its clients from large and small corporations, and another indicates that trade associations and medium-sized companies make up a small percentage. Clients are involved with marketing, research and development, advertising, and planning activities.

Advertising is very limited. Only one service received some press coverage in a major library publication—because of a debate on library service for a fee vs. free library service. Another service was listed in *Information Manager* in a "Products and Services" section. None take out advertisements, and two have promotional brochures, which tend to reflect the interests of the parent company rather than those of the services.

The internal services use in-house libraries, but one uses online databases 80 percent of the time. One service has a very large in-house collection of more than 22,000 books, 1,100 periodicals, and 2,500 industry files. All receive requests directly at least 90 percent of the time, the majority via telephone. Mail requests account for 10–30 percent, and one reports 20 percent in-person requests.

One service is instituting fixed fees; the others offer retainer accounts. All three are acutely aware of other fee-based information services and look to the larger firms for ideas. Only one of the internal services has implemented quality control standards to measure effectiveness.

Chase Information Center is the only one of the three that has undertaken much external promotion. One news story featured the headline "Chase Manhattan Bank Is in the Library Business." A brief news release was sent to *Library Journal* in mid-1978 and announced "research and library services to the business public on a fee basis."[2] A special brochure described the center and detailed its work. In addition to searching, document delivery, and other services common to fee-based firms, the Chase Information Center publishes *Biz-dex*™, a monthly abstract of 125 articles and books drawn from more than 300 periodicals. All of the services are offered on a retainer basis or on a payment per use basis with monthly billing. Retainer customers are offered a rate of $30 per hour for searching, the lowest of any major information service, possibly because it is not profitable. Competitors—for example, FIND—are already engaging the same potential clients using professional marketing staffs, highly sophisticated promotional literature, and frequent in-person sales calls.

FREE-LANCERS—INFO/MOTION AND INFORMATION RESOURCES

A number of individual information services in business in the mid-1970s have virtually disappeared from the fee-based information service scene. The two services that are profiled here, as well as others that have survived, may have followed the advice of pioneers in the 1970s. Many free-lance librarians are still active in alternative library movements, free press, such as Library Free Press and Booklegger, and networks such as Women Library Workers and ALA Social Responsibility Round Tables.[3] The following profiles discuss two independent firms that have successfully provided highly personalized and specialized services. Both are owned by women who advocate improving relations between librarians and information brokers. (See also Chapter 8 for more information on the free-lancers).

INFO/MOTION was founded in 1976 in Lenox, Mass., shortly after the Syracuse workshop. Director Barbara Whyte Felicetti has written articles on information brokering for library journals and has addressed the misconceptions of the information broker and the librarian as enemies. She believes that "the role of the information broker is to supplement existing reference services whether in public libraries, corporate libraries, or community information centers."[4] She has also been active in Associated Information Managers and has conducted workshops on getting started in small business (such as at the information conference NICE IV, May 1980).

INFO/MOTION's services include information on demand, computerized literature searching, research, bibliographics, library organization, current awareness programs, indexing, and abstracting. Her clients are large and medium corporations from New York City and Albany areas involved in marketing activities, as well as individual professionals.

INFO/MOTION does not aggressively advertise, but ads have been placed in local newspapers. The director relies on word of mouth to create her own publicity campaign and continues to be an outspoken independent information broker.

Another outspoken information broker is Susan Klement, who established Information Resources in 1969; it is one of the oldest information services in Canada. She is responsible for the pioneering concept of "alternatives in librarianship." Says Klement, "a demand, as well as a need, for education in this field exists; it remains for more library schools to recognize this fact." She has taught graduate courses at the University of Toronto and Kent State library schools.

Information Resources was the first to offer innovative workshops in "alternatives in librarianship." These workshops have attracted large audiences. The course is intended to "indicate the enormous potential of our profession, not to suggest that people leave the field for better things . . . encouraging libraries to fill alternative positions and remain oriented to the profession will be of benefit to libraries in many ways."[5]

In addition to seminars and workshops, Information Resources offers information on demand, literature searching, bibliography and directory compilation, document delivery, indexing and abstracting, report writing, editing, and thesaurus construction. Clients include all sizes of firms, government agencies, and individuals (authors, lawyers, market researchers, and others).

Susan Klement has stated that there is an infinite market for personalized research. Her interest in research began during her years in an academic bookstore. She does not send out printed brochures, but believes in telling people about her work. She has sent out resumes that quote her rates at $50 per hour per person. An innovative independent broker, she has compiled a bibliography on "alternatives in librarianship." She is also active on speaking tours in the U.S. and Canada.

Both of these free-lancers are active in professional associations and educational workshops to aid the would-be free-lance librarian.

NOTES

1. In 1979–80, seminars began on a bimonthly basis.
2. "At Chase Manhattan Bank: Library Service for a Fee," *Library Journal,* August 1978, p. 1476.
3. *Bulletin of American Society of Information Science,* 2 (December 1976), 20.
4. Barbara Whyte Felicetti, "Information for a Fee and Information for Free." *Public Library Quarterly,* 1 (Spring 1979), 18.
5. Susan Klement, "A Graduate Course on Alternatives in Librarianship"—draft proposal.

8

THE FREE-LANCER

The state of California has long had the highest number of free-lance librarians and fee-based information services. The free-lance information broker phenomenon is believed to have begun on the West Coast in the San Francisco Bay Area. Several individuals who started their businesses in the late 1960s and early 1970s were also the founding members of the "Revolting Librarians" movement of that era. Both *Booklegger Press,* a collective publication, and *Synergy,* formerly published by the San Francisco Public Library, chronicle this period in articles written by the pioneers of fee-based information services on the West Coast. Women Library Workers, a national organization headquartered in Berkeley, California, emerged in the mid-1970s to cater to the concerns of the new library professionals. Sex and salary discrimination in libraries were the major issues, and many individuals went into business for themselves to earn a better than competitive library wage. Other factors that contributed to the growth of information brokering in the Bay Area are the social support system and downward mobility indigenous to that region. California is known for its tolerance of nontraditional, newly created, or alternative work styles.

Additional free-lancers appeared during the late 1970s, some attributed to Proposition 13, which increased the number of unemployed librarians already in the marketplace. Two information services, however, were formed in 1979 when the original partnership of a successful service was dissolved. Several of the

California free-lance information specialists contract with one another and have formed a close-knit alliance. Nearly all the principals who were surveyed know of their colleagues in the field who are in the same region.

Of the nine California information services that responded, six are located in metropolitan areas of San Francisco and Los Angeles. Five are in the same cities where larger information services operate. Several respondents feel that the business climate of the San Francisco Bay Area was a major factor for embarking on their ventures.

The 22 information free-lancers who responded from other states have more recent origins. In New York, 4 of the 6 who replied were established in 1976 or later, largely due to an outgrowth of the movement for alternative curricula in library schools during the mid-1970s. More students were being exposed to on-line applications, information marketing, and information science in library schools, notably the Syracuse University School of Information Studies (so called since 1974). Only one of these information services is located in New York City; several are in upper New York State. Moreover, at least 25 indexers in New York were ineligible for inclusion in this study. Therefore, New York has the second highest number of fee-based information services.

Three brokers are located in Pennsylvania; two in Washington, D.C., Massachusetts, and Colorado; and one each in Oregon, Utah, Nevada, Missouri, Kansas, Florida, and Vermont. Of these, seven are in greater metropolitan areas. Twenty-seven of the respondents in this category were established in the 1970s, four in the 1960s, and one in the 1950s.

Of the 31 free-lancers who responded (see list at end of this chapter), initial capitalization for 19 was $1,000 or less; 9 invested under $10,000; 2 did not disclose figures. Sixteen employ part-time personnel. One employs library school students and paraprofessional librarians for additional staffing; 2 mentioned part-time clerical support staff; and one specified using only other information specialists.

A large majority (23) have library science degrees, and 12 indicate various combinations of library degree, subject degree, and library experience. The backgrounds mentioned are computer and information science, on-line searching, public information training, book publishing, management, journalism, art and architecture, international studies, genealogy and local history, research, and consulting.

Only 3 prefer the title information broker solely; 6 use information specialist, 4 information service, and 2 library consultant; 10 use a combination of two or more of the terms, and 2 said they used all. Additional terms include library research service, information consultant, management consultant, consulting information specialist, editorial and visual consulting service, and genealogical researcher. One New Yorker uses information broker; another said that he is an information broker operating an information service. Some of those surveyed use terms that potential clients might readily understand, and the terminology depends on the situation.

Independent information specialists are fairly active in several library and nonlibrary-related associations, most (13) in both the Special Libraries Association and the American Library Association. Seven belong to the American Society of Information Science and five to the Information Industry Association (4 of them in the subgroup, Association of Information Managers). At least a dozen other groups were listed by over half of the respondents. They range from state and regional associations (library associations, chambers of commerce, and such), to professional societies for marketing and advertising (American Marketing Association, Direct Mail Marketing Association, Mail Advertising Services Association), management and consulting (National Management Association, Institute of Management Consultants, Associated Independent Consultants), and technology (Association for Educational Communication Technology). Special interest groups include the American Society of Picture Professionals, Association of Professional Genealogists, Association of Asian Studies, Media Alliance, Women Entrepreneurs, and Association of Female Executives.

A large number of the respondents provide consulting services (30), research services (28), and bibliographies (24). Twenty undertake manual searching; 20 offer indexing; 17 provide document delivery, information on demand, and on-line searching; 16 conduct seminars and workshops; and 13 produce analytical reports. Less popular services are publications (11), selective dissemination of information (SDI) (9), translating (5), and market reports (5). Additional services include picture research, editing and records management, public relations, management consulting, abstracting, architectural programming, library space planning, designing information retrieval systems, and creating/maintaining information centers.

The number of independent information specialists who provide on-line searching is an indication of the trend of the 1970s. As discussed in Chapter 3, the number of individual subscribers to on-line retrieval systems is increasing, thus decreasing the demand for services providing only on-line searching and producing competition from non-information specialists.

Most subject areas are covered by the independent information services, although 17 noted business and 15, social science. Only 9 deal in the science-technology area and 7 in the health sciences. Additional subject coverage includes genealogy (4), government (2), energy and environment (2), art and architecture (2), law (1), and East Asian affairs (1).

Clientele for the independent information services covers a wide range. The majority of clients are in the private sector, from 75–100 percent, although 2 services have percentages as low as 25–30. Only 4 services receive more than 70 percent of their business from the public sector, and of these, 2 indicate 80 and 100 percent from nonprofit organizations (research institutions, trade associations, libraries). Small business comprises 50 percent or less of the total business for 14 of the services. Only 6 indicate percentages above 50 percent for small business. Only 5 services report 65–70 percent of their business from large corporations; 10 indicate a 5–50 percent range from the corporate sector. Government provides an average of 15 percent for most of the services. Interestingly enough, government is not a client for any of the California-based firms. Only one service reports 70 percent of its business from government, primarily for the editing of government publications. Nonprofit organizations have the widest range—1–100 percent. Two report 100 percent from research institutions, trade associations, and libraries/information centers; 11 report percentages of 30 or less, and 3 as high as 75–80 percent. Individuals, publishers, authors, filmmakers, designers, and lawyers constitute other clients. Two information services report 90–100 percent business from this group, which includes scholarly research and family history. One service reports 10 percent of its business from graduate students, primarily for on-line searching.

The rate of repeat business for independent information services is relatively high, with an average of 50 percent. However, 4 firms indicate rates of 60–90 percent and one reports only 5 percent repeat business. To a large extent, clientele for these services is local as opposed to the larger services' national and worldwide clients. Seventeen respondents indicate rates of 50 percent or above for clients in their own communities, and of these, 3 indicate 100 percent and 4 note 90–95 percent for local business. State and regional clientele varies, with the majority reporting an average of 20 percent. One, however, reports 100 percent statewide. National clientele range from 15–99 percent, with 6 services reporting 50 percent or greater. Only 5 indicate having international clientele (1–10 percent), and one service, which specializes in Far Eastern studies, claims 50 percent of its business abroad.

Clients are engaged in a variety of activities. Ten firms have clients in marketing departments, and 3 indicate over 50 percent of their clients as such. Clients for 14 firms come from research and development departments, and 9 have 50 percent or less of their clients engaged in those areas. One Californian who specializes in systems design has 100 percent of her clients from this group. Administrators constitute business for 14 of the independent information services, but the percentages are all under 50 percent. One information consultant, who specializes in systems analysis and design, works totally with management. Additional client activities listed by 19 of the services include family research (2 reported 100 percent), publishing (3), personal research (2), communications industries (1 service reported 100 percent), education (2), writing (2), manufacturing (1), banking (1), legal research (2), architectural planning (2), editing (1), and translating (1). This data indicates that independent services cater to special interest groups with specialized information needs. Free-lancers provide custom research and information services for their varied clientele, and this gives them a "cutting edge" in the industry.

The majority of requests for research and information services are received directly; 23 respondents indicate 90–100 percent of their requests this way. Only one receives 100 percent indirectly through corporate librarians and information center personnel; 10 others indicate 30 percent or below for indirect requests.

The independent information services unanimously agree that word-of-mouth is one of the most effective means of generating business—23 choose it as the most effective tool; 9 think it equally as effective as other techniques. Other marketing tools include conferences, professional meetings, and direct mail (18 each); seminars, workshops, and the like (14); publications, directory listings (10); sales calls (9); newspaper and journal advertising (7 each); and editorial coverage in specialized press (7). Only 2 have taken out Yellow Pages advertising, and one produces radio advertisements, but none indicate these as cost-effective practices. One reports high visibility through articles for professional journals.

Very few of the independent information specialists have invested in substantial public relations efforts. Brochures are usually inexpensive, double-folded pamphlets with limited graphic design. Thirteen respondents have not produced any business materials—brochures, business cards, stationery, and the like. Perhaps the high quantity of repeat business and client referrals has eliminated the need for additional marketing practices for this group. The key to a successful operation is the development of close personal rapport among information specialists and their clients. Personal contacts must be established in order to solicit business. In addition, personality plays an important role, and these individuals must be able to communicate effectively, have a sense of business know-how, act poised, and aggressively promote their services. Since there is a high mortality rate for small businesses, these factors are crucial.

Most of the projects involving the independent information services are long term, and the average length of a contract is two years. Twelve respondents receive fewer than 20 requests per month, and only seven receive over 100 per year. The highest number (500 per year) is reported by a New York firm, which provides a substantial number of on-line search services as well as customized bibliographies to nonprofit organizations (65 percent are libraries and information centers). Average turnaround time varies, usually from several weeks to several years with the exception of on-line searching.

Nearby libraries are the most frequently cited source for answering requests for 28 of the respondents. Of these, 7 report utilization of 50 percent or more. On-line databases are popular among 17 services, with 4 indicating usage of 50 percent or greater. Most services are located in individuals' homes, and 22 depend on in-house collections and personal resources. Only 4, however, report usage as high as 75–80 percent, and the average range is 5–20 percent; 22 also telephone experts for information, but the reported percentages are in the 5–25 range. One service uses this source for over half its requests. Six subcontract with other information services for the following: on-line searching (2), document delivery (2), translating (1), and additional research (1). The average use of other information services is 10 percent, although one reports 5 percent and another as high as 25 percent. Additional sources include primary, on-site, original research (4); county archives and historical collections (2); photo agencies and picture archives (1). One individual uses clients' resources 75 percent of the time, and one conducts personal interviews 10 percent of the time. None of the services report any restrictions placed on their use of nearby libraries.

The majority of requests are received via telephone, and 15 receive telephone inquiries 60 percent of the time. Mail requests are received by 21; only 5 indicate percentages as high as 70–95 percent. One, who reports 95 percent, is a genealogist and receives inquiries worldwide due to notices she places in American and foreign journals. Only one receives teletype requests. In-person requests are very common among this group; 21 receive them—3 as high as 95–100 percent, with the average 25–30 percent. Only 10 keep records of the proportion of requests they receive through each channel.

Pricing strategies are less rigid than for the larger information services. One specialist says that the firm takes any reasonable offer; one genealogist accepts patron donations instead of fixed fees (whatever the patron wishes to pay). Nineteen firms negotiate their fees; 13 utilize a cost plus predetermined profit margin as a basis; and 3 set rates based on competitor's charges. One uses fixed-price contracts and another charges "consultant's fees." The majority are in favor of a sliding scale system of negotiation; one reports losing business from a set hourly rate. Fees average $10–$15 per hour, although one genealogist charges $5 per hour and 6 have set daily rates ranging from $100–$250. The low rates contrast dramatically with the $35 per hour average for small and medium-sized information services and the $50–$75 per hour for the larger firms. This low rate is attributed to minimal overhead expenses for the independent services.

Clients, for the most part, are billed per job. Three services request payment in advance, two require deposits of 30 percent or more, and two offer retainer accounts in addition to the billing option. One offers student discounts on fees paid in advance for on-line searches.

Twenty-one of the independent information firms provide free referral services, usually five minutes worth of advice, over the phone. Percentages of operating expenses of billings are reported by only seven and range from 0.05 to 45–55 (one reports 100 percent).

When asked if they knew of other information services offering similar services, 15 said no and 16 said yes. When asked if they considered themselves in competition with these other services, however, only one said yes. One free-lancer considers other information specialists as "colleagues in the same market-place," and another claims that more cooperation (subcontracting) exists than competition. The few information services that were named as competitors include medium-sized firms in metropolitan areas.

Only four of these firms assume legal liability for the accuracy of the information they provide, and of these, one is a genealogist who relies on certified historical data. One on-line searcher advises clients against the potential omission of documents in a literature search.

Client referral, solicitation of feedback, repeat business, and sales volume are the most frequently cited ways of measuring the effectiveness of these information services. With the high rate of repeat business, it is to be expected that client feedback would be of critical importance. All the respondents indicate strong feelings of responsibility toward their clients, and one says that the customer pays only if he or she is satisfied with the end product. A California information specialist measures effectiveness by personal "peace of mind." Two cite internal audits of their services (one by turnaround time and another by evaluation).

A significant number of the free-lancers plan new publishing ventures (directories, newsletters, reports). One will enter database production, and another wants to produce a computer-based, in-house index. Others mention conducting seminars or workshops for special client groups.

The independent specialists' perspective of the future for the industry as a whole is quite diverse. Most are acutely aware of the trend toward more specialized information services. One remarked that "there will always be a market for personalized service . . . it's a matter of educating the public." Three specialists located in urban areas feel that the demand for information brokering will be nonexistent in the next 15–20 years when homes and businesses have their own information utilities. Another is concerned with maintenance of professional standards and the contribution of library schools. Another predicts that "libraries will be forced to change their mode of operation due to costs and technologies." For one experienced free-lancer, six assets are necessary for success—competence, capital, contacts, patience, willpower, and an innovative outlook.

Free-lance survey respondents:
    Acquire Information (Palo Alto, Calif.)
    Golden V. Adams (Provo, Utah)

Ruth E. Carsch (San Francisco, Calif.)

Loren Fay (Moravia, N.Y.)

Marianne Griffin and Associates (Lawrence, Kans.)

Jane Huang (Delmar, N.Y.)

Deborah Hunt (Reno, Nev.)

In-Fact (Rensselaerville, N.Y.)

THE INFO-MART (Santa Barbara, Calif.)

Information and Research International/The East Asia Research Institute (Washington, D.C.)

Information Control (Rutland, Vt.)

Information Professionals (Denver, Colo.)

Information Resource Consultants (St. Louis, Mo.)

Information Services and Research (Syracuse, N.Y.)

Information Yield (Syracuse, N.Y.)

INFO/MOTION (Lenox, Mass.)

Infosense Consulting Services (Narberth, Pa.)

Richard L. King (Cerritos, Calif.)

Library Information Services (Oakland, Calif.)

William Needham (Tallahassee, Fla.)

Northwest Information Enterprises (Beaverton, Oreg.)

On-Hand Advisory Service (Marblehead, Mass.)

Organization Plus (Denver, Colo.)

Posts' Information Service (Philadelphia, Pa.)

Martha A. Powers (Berkeley, Calif.)

Research Reports (N.Y.C.)

Dawn M. Saunders (Manhattan Beach, Calif.)

Doris P. Shalley (Washington Crossing, Pa.)

Patricia K. Smith (Washington, D.C.)

Umbrella Associates (Glendale, Calif.)

Barbara Wurf (Los Angeles, Calif.)

BASIC QUESTIONS AND ANSWERS

Q. Where are the majority of free-lance information services located?

A. California.

Q. What kinds of services do free-lancers provide?

A. Consulting, research, bibliographies, manual searching, indexing, document delivery, information-on-demand, on-line searching.

Q. Who are the clients for free-lancers?
A. The majority are in the private sector.
Q. What do free-lancers name as their most effective means of generating business?
A. Word-of-mouth.
Q. How do free-lancers answer most requests?
A. From nearby libraries.
Q. How does the free-lancer receive most requests?
A. Via telephone.

9

FEE-BASED INFORMATION
SERVICES ABROAD

The primary focus of this chapter is on fee-based information services in the United Kingdom, since the U.K. seems to be the leader in growth for such European firms. There are, however, several companies in other countries that provide fee-based information services, such as the French firm of SVP (see Chapter 6). The listing of information brokers and consultants in *Information Market Place 1978–1979* includes more than 25 companies in Austria, Belgium, England, France, Germany, the Netherlands, Spain, Switzerland, and Yugoslavia. *The Journal of Fee-Based Information Services* (1979–.) lists additional English, Australian, Icelandic, and Japanese services.[1]

Most of the European companies are members of the European Association of Information Services (EUSIDIC), and on a national level, they belong to special library associations, such as Aslib (formerly the Association of Library Information Bureaus) in the U.K. As in the United States, there are no organizations that fully represent the European fee-based information service industry. With the establishment of the European Group of the Information Industry Association and the European Information Providers Association in late 1979, this situation is changing.

Services operating in Europe can be classified as:

Set up expressly as fee-based information services (such as SVP in Paris, NPM Information Services in London).

Government or other official organizations seeking additional income (such as Institute for Industrial Research and Standards—IIRS—in Ireland and Centre for Scientific and Technical Information and Documentation of the Netherlands Organization for Applied Scientific Research—CID-TNO—in Holland).

Evolved from market research or management consultancy companies.

Started by individual entrepreneurs who resigned or retired from larger companies.

The range of services provided by these organizations is varied. Compared with the United States, on-line searching often has a secondary role because of the high telecommunications costs when using U.S.-based host computers and the apparent lack of databases covering European business affairs. EURONET-DIANE service, which will offer European databases at substantially lower telecommunications costs, is changing this situation. The Direct Information Access Network (DIANE) is a "project conceived, sponsored and designed by the Commission of the European Communities to serve the needs of business and government institutions throughout the nine member states and to meet the requirements of European information users."[2] The system became available in March 1980 with 15 hosts and some 90 databases and works in cooperation with the European Postal and Telecommunications Administrations (PTT's) of the nine countries.

Fee-based information services have to operate in an environment where information is readily available. The economic situation in Europe is creating an increasing demand for business and commercial information. Companies seeking technical information and finding their in-house resources inadequate, often turn to research associations or government libraries and departments. When business information (product, market, company, legal, economic data) is required, there is a growing tendency to contact a fee-based service.

Fee-based information services in the U.K. are commonly called "information consultancies" and their principals, "information consultants." As can be seen from the listing of U.K. services in Appendix 3, only a few can be regarded as "information brokers" in the American sense. With two major exceptions, virtually all British information services are small companies with fewer than five full-time employees. Most of the companies are located in London to take advantage of the numerous special libraries. Excluding research and trade associations, there are probably no more than a dozen companies whose sole activity is to provide fee-based information services. The two largest services, the Financial Times Business Information Service and the Times Business Information and Marketing Intelligence Unit, have evolved from existing internal operations. The Warwick Statistics Service is another large firm funded mainly by the University of Warwick.

At present, competition from research associations and publicly funded libraries is keeping individual information specialists out of the field. The individuals who are listed in the *Journal of Fee-Based Information Services* have specialized services, such as genealogical research, technical translations, publications consulting.

Advertising for fee-based information services in England is limited, and Yellow Pages listings are practically nonexistent. The standard directory is the *Aslib Directory of Special Libraries in the U.K.*, last revised in 1976–77. The membership list of Aslib is helpful since the subject index has an entry for "Commercial Information and Translation Services" and "Consultants." The 1979–80 list has 40 entries, but many of these are commercial publishers, such as the Institute for Scientific Information, or on-line services such as InfoLine. The Yellow Pages are used by very few services mainly because of the problem of deciding which subject headings are most appropriate.

The majority of clients in the U.K. are acquired by word-of-mouth and they tend to be major companies or their subsidiaries. Other clients include trade associations, banks, public authorities, and marketing consultants. There is often strong geographical bias; many clients of the Warwick Statistics Service, for example, are engineering firms located within 50 miles of Warwick. The majority of information services are engaged in "desk research" or manual searching and research activities. About half offer on-line searching, and a typical search is charged out at $120–$180, unless subsidized. Other services include document delivery, consulting (such as designing library and information systems), seminars, newsletter publications, and translations.

Information-gathering techniques are focused on the resources of nearby libraries rather than on in-house collections or on-line databases. Most of the information services belong to Aslib or the Institute for Information Scientists (IIS); this allows them privileges at other member libraries. Many rely on public and business libraries for a major part of the time and the British Library Lending Division for retrieval of specialized documents. Free-lance translators and agencies are frequently subcontracted by the fee-based services.

The fees charged vary widely. Some firms, such as the Financial Times, The Times, and Warwick Statistics Service, have deposit accounts against which work is charged. These deposits typically range from £125 to £250 ($300–$600). The average hourly rate ranges between £20 and £30 ($50–$80). As in any service industry, the largest cost is salaries, and most overheads are related to the number of employees.

The market size and turnover rate are difficult to determine because of the diversification of information services that might appear within research associations or large organizations. An abundance of information services in the public sector—public library, university library, research associations—is the major reason for the low growth rate of fee-based services. These services face stiff competition from public and university libraries as well as research associations. The U.K. has an excellent public library system, and several of its libraries have developed a wide range of services to meet the needs of local industries. These libraries are mainly located in the large industrial cities of Birmingham, Liverpool, Manchester, Newcastle, and Sheffield. In London, the Westminster and Camden Libraries have similar facilities. The City Business Library of London, funded by the City and the Corporation of London, provides excellent reference services and is used heavily by clients throughout the U.K. None of these libraries charges for the information. The exception is for on-line search services, in which case only the direct costs are passed on. Rates for on-line services average £30 ($70) per hour. The scope of these operations is usually limited, but the volume is steady.

Universities and polytechnical institutions also offer on-line search services. Survey findings[3] presented to the SCONUL (Standing Committee of National University Libraries) On-Line Services Seminar, in June 1979, indicated that more than 70 percent of U.K. university libraries use on-line retrieval systems, a percentage that is rapidly increasing. On-line services are provided primarily to academic and postgraduate researchers, the majority free of charge. Few libraries have more than two trained searchers, and many are in the developmental stages of integrating on-line retrieval into their regular information services. More than 50 percent of the responding libraries have annual on-line budgets in excess of £2000 ($4000).

Since the late 1920s, research associations in the U.K. have provided centralized research facilities for groups of companies from particular industry sectors. Until the early 1970s, these associations received extensive government support, but this was withdrawn and the associations had to adopt a much higher proportion of contract research. The Rubber and Plastics Association, the British Nonferrous Metals Technology Centre, the Welding Institute, and the Shirley Institute are the leading exponents. All of these research associations have produced on-line databases that are available on U.S. host computers. Other research and trade associations, such as The Metals Society, have well-developed information services that they offer primarily to their members. Due to rising costs and other economic factors, several research associations and a few of the trade groups now offer information services to nonmembers on a fee-paying basis.

Aslib is another example of a research association that provides information services to more than 3,000 corporate members in the U.K. and 77 other countries. Many government, academic, industrial, and special libraries belong to Aslib and subscribe to its services, which include referral and inquiry, on-line search, and consulting. In addition, Aslib offers training courses, annual conferences, and seminars. The Aslib Information Department accesses various computer databases, charging a fixed hourly rate of £25 ($60).[4] This search service is available only to Aslib members.

Increasing cutbacks in government funding and public spending may restrict libraries and research associations from providing low cost services. Martin White, spokesperson for the European Group of the Information Industry Association, commented:

> The competition is not just the problem of combatting a free service, but the general assumption throughout the U.K. that information should be free, and freely available. Two developments may change this position. Firstly, the cutbacks by the Conservative Government during 1979–80 may force libraries to start recovering some of the costs of providing reference services. Secondly, the advent of Prestel (Viewdata) may also hasten the awareness that information does cost money, and that cost and value are not necessarily synonymous. Apart from other economic factors, the major barrier to the development of fee-based information services in the U.K. is the cost of educating potential customers in the use of these services. With the high costs of

printing and mailing brochures, there is little an individual company can do to materially affect the level of awareness of the
advantages of using fee-based information services.[5]

In his report to the British Library, White (then director of NPM
Information Services) recommended that information services in
the U.K. be supported as an undeveloped or embryonic industry.
He also indicated, at the 1980 Aslib/IIS/LA Joint Conference, that
there are some 650,000 registered companies in the U.K., of
which at least 100,000 could derive benefit from having improved
access to information brokers. He suggests that Aslib, in conjunction with the British Library, adopt a greater educational and
promotional role by establishing a forum for the industry.

A study of 40 fee-based information services was undertaken
in July 1977 by Christine Birks, a doctoral student at the Centre
for Information Science at the City University.[6] This is the only
documented report of the information service industry in the
U.K. The author surveyed and interviewed the principals of "on-
demand services" on behalf of the British Library. The study was
apparently motivated by the belief that financial pressures would
cause many libraries to earn income by selling services. Although
several of the survey respondents work on their own, the majority
are backed by large organizations. Most offer both business and
technical information services and customers seem concentrated
in large firms in the private sector. Word-of-mouth, rather than
promotion, was viewed as the most effective means of generating
business. The respondents generally expect competition to become keener, with a definite trend toward specialization. Birks'
conclusion is still opposite to the present U.K. situation:

> Competition in this field can only become fiercer and services
> which have not investigated their markets or persist with uncon-
> sidered or unsystematic management and assessment will be in-
> creasingly vulnerable to the incursions of their more dynamic
> fellows.[7]

Like many of the American information services surveyed,
forecasts by U.K. services are optimistic for the future of the
industry. Many U.K. services have adopted the terms "information brokerage" or "information broking" in their promotional
literature. Several principals have expressed a desire for greater
reciprocity with North American information services, and they
also look forward to establishing a greater network among
themselves.

CLOSE-UP OF A U.K. FEE-BASED INFORMATION SERVICE

This profile of a typical U.K. information service was brought to the authors' attention during a meeting of information brokers at the annual Information Industry Association Conference (NICE III). Martin White, former director of this service, is currently chairperson of the European Committee of the Information Industry Association.

New Product Management (NPM) Information Services was established in 1977 as a division of a privately owned management consulting firm. The firm was founded in the 1800s as a patent agency, and it evolved over the years into a consulting service for industries seeking to develop new products and/or new markets. NPM offers a wide range of information services and products, including market research, consulting, information-on-request, document delivery, on-line and manual searching, bibliographies, analytical reports, translations, and publications. A proprietary databank, called PLIBANK™, enables searching of manufacturing and marketing license offers and requests. The Information Desk is staffed by three full-time personnel, two with M.L.S. degrees. Business and finance are the areas primarily covered, and specialized services include patent information searching and tracking (Company Watch and Patent Watch). The Information Audit service provides analyses and evaluations of management information systems for those companies without professional information staff. The Information Desk is an information-on-demand service that provides technical and commercial information for industry. Many of its customers are retainer clientele of the NPM Consulting Group. The majority are large and medium-sized industrial corporations in the private sector. Over 90 percent of these clients are national; the remainder are international companies. Half are engaged in marketing and half in research and development. There is a high rate of repeat business, due to the number of retainer clientele maintained. External business accounts for 30 percent of the volume of sales.

The most effective marketing tool is word-of-mouth or client referral. Other techniques employed by NPM include sales calls, direct mailings, conference attendance, editorial coverage in specialized press, and promotion through its newsletters and publications. NPM publishes *Information Management*,[8] a monthly publication of recent developments in the information industry, and *Information Surveys,* an irregular report series on topical subjects (Prestel, word processing, on-line retrieval, and so on). An attractive brochure (part of which is shown in this section) was designed for NPM Information Services.

Seventy percent of the requests are received by telephone; 8 of 10 are direct inquiries. Only 20 percent of all requests received are by mail and fewer via teletype or in person. A small percentage (20) is received indirectly through corporate librarians. Nearby libraries (public, university, research) are heavily used (50 percent) for answering queries. On-line databases and in-house collections account for 20 percent and 10 percent respectively. NPM also has a small internal collection of management texts and journals, but has access to several specialized libraries in the London vicinity. Subcontracting with other information services in the United Kingdom and abroad enables NPM to gather data for 20 percent of its requests. Pricing is based on a cost plus predetermined profit margin as well as on a negotiated basis. The hourly rate of £25–£35 ($50–$80) is competitively priced within both British and American marketplaces. Clients for the "quick quote" or "current awareness service" are billed per job unless they are retainer-account customers. Research services are also billed per job, but separately from retainer accounts. Since only secondary or previously published information is supplied by NPM, it does not assume liability for accuracy of the data. Seminars and workshops on information management and information for business are planned for the future.

Competition exists on a local level, but not to a large extent since the U.K. marketplace is relatively unexploited. NPM has goals for 25–40 percent growth rates through the mid-1980s.

BASIC QUESTIONS AND ANSWERS

Q. Where are foreign fee-based information services located?
A. Austria, Belgium, England, France, Germany, the Netherlands, Spain, Switzerland, and Yugoslavia.
Q. To what organizations do these foreign firms belong?
A. Mainly to the European Association of Information Services (EUSIDIC) and the Association of Information and Dissemination Centers (ASIDIC).
Q. What is the common name for these services in England?
A. Information consultancies and information consultants.
Q. Where are English information firms listed?
A. The annual *Aslib Directory of Special Libraries in the U.K.*

Information

Desk

From time to time you will be faced with the need to make a decision on the basis of inadequate information. In the present economic climate there is no room for an uneducated guess, no opportunity for a second chance. Our INFORMATION DESK, staffed by qualified information retrieval specialists, can supply you with information on any subject relating to your company's business interests.

We have access to a wide range of specialised sources of information and computer-based information services. Our network of contacts throughout the USA and Europe can often provide invaluable 'on-the-spot' research on companies and market opportunities. With these resources we can quickly and cost-effectively supply information on:

PRODUCTS 'Are there any energy-saving products developed in the USA that I could manufacture in the UK?'

MARKETS 'What is the projected market for videorecorders in Europe over the next five years?'

COMPANIES 'I need a list of companies with interests in the US leisure industry'

TECHNOLOGIES 'What is the current position of optical fibre technology?'

PATENTS 'Can you provide a monthly survey of patents on electric vehicles?'

We can undertake searches of the published literature, and provide an up-dating service at regular intervals. Our COMPANY WATCH and PATENT WATCH services can give you vital advance warning of the business interests of your competitors.

INFORMATION DESK staff could also solve your next information problem. Can you afford not to have our ex-directory telephone number available?

NOTES

1. Kelly Warnken, *Journal of Fee-Based Information Services,* supplement sections in vol. I, nos. 4, 6, and vol. II, nos. 1, 2, 1979–80.
2. 1980 EURONET-DIANE brochure.
3. This survey was carried out in April 1978 by John Akeroyd (City of London Polytechnic) and Allen Foster (Sheffield City Polytechnic). "On-line Information Services in U.K. Academic Libraries," *On-Line Review* 3 (June 1979), 195–204.
4. Aslib Information Department, 1980 brochure.
5. Personal communication.
6. Christine I. Birks, *Information Services in the Market Place* (London: The British Library (Research and Development Report, no. 5430, 1978).
7. Ibid., p. 53.
8. Available at subscription price of £24 ($60).

10

FEE-BASED INFORMATION SERVICES AND THE LIBRARY

Fee-based information services are seen by some as a threat to the tradition of American free library service. This perception is due, in part, to a lack of understanding about the information service industry, but it is, to a greater degree, a reflection of the dramatic changes occurring in information gathering, transfer, and utilization.

One of the events that fueled concern by librarians was the Information Industry Association's (IIA) testimony before the National Commission on Libraries and Information Science (NCLIS) in April 1973. IIA board chairman Eugene Garfield, president of the Institute for Scientific Information, told the commission that "user-based charges must inevitably prevail."[1]

Paul Zurkowski, executive director of IIA, tried to place Garfield's comments in context, not long after the NCLIS hearings, by saying of the user charges suggestion that "in certain specialized areas where the available information services are very specialized or expensive, a for-profit library might well develop, thereby relieving some competition for the ever-diminishing public resources available for libraries."[2]

These statements are in sharp contrast with the view of many librarians that all libraries and information services must be free to all users as a matter of right. Fay Blake and Edith Perlmutter wrote a response to both Garfield and Zurkowski in which they said, "Several recent developments in the world of American libraries seem to foreshadow an ominous trend toward a new concept of library service. The concept is translated into a variety of proposals—the 'information supermarket,' 'libraries for profit,' 'user fees,' 'user-based charges'—but what's really being proposed is an elimination of tax-supported library services."[3]

Richard De Gennaro, director of libraries at the University of Pennsylvania, commented in early 1979 that "the battle lines are being drawn for a great debate over the emotionally and politically charged issue of how libraries are to be funded in the coming decades."[4] He expressed the view that "much of the heat and misunderstanding comes from the very different images that the words 'libraries' and 'information' invoke in the various protagonists and the context or frame of reference in which they use them."[5] He argued that for-profit libraries ought to be accepted "to serve the special needs of industrial, commercial, and other users who are willing and able to pay for special computerized information services."[6] In addition, he acknowledged that in most libraries "the amount of service given depends on staffing levels, time available and the status of the requestor. Most libraries decline to do time-consuming literature searches, report writing, or translation, and refer these requests to other persons or agencies who will perform the service for a fee."[7]

De Gennaro identified photocopying and computerized bibliographic services as two areas in which "free libraries have been charging their patrons for a number of years." He urged moderation in this way: "In sum, different libraries can adopt different policies on the question of user charges for special services depending on their own local budgets and circumstances. There is no need for uniform or inflexible policies, and librarians can implement these peripheral charges on an ad hoc basis without embracing the concept of the user-supported library or the information supermarket as a matter of political faith or economic inevitability."[8]

The debate continued despite the efforts of pragmatists in librarianship and the information industry. In 1979, an information specialist devoted another article to the subject under the title "Information for Fee and Information for Free: The Information Broker and the Public Librarian." The author addressed the misconception that the information broker would replace the public library and the public librarian. She argued that "the role of the information broker is to supplement existing reference services whether they are located in public libraries, corporate libraries, or community information centers."[9]

The Library Association of the City University of New York (LACUNY), a professional association of librarians employed by the City University of New York, sponsored a conference that same year to discuss the conflict between libraries and fee-based information services. The chairperson of the conference said in her introductory remarks:

> While many librarians reject with a sense of moral indignation the suggestion that user fees be levied, the information brokers have stepped into a vacuum created by emerging demand for services that most libraries are unable or unwilling to provide.[10]

The compatability of the library and a fee-based information service is best illustrated by the existence of the latter in several major public libraries throughout the United States (Cleveland, Dallas, Denver, Minneapolis, and Tulsa). Among the oldest of such services in a public library is Inform, the nonprofit research service of the Minneapolis Public Library and Information Center. The charter of Inform states: "The purpose of Inform is to offer, on a fee basis, an information service to anyone contracting for the service. The objective of Inform is to provide the user with access to library resources and professional skills to a degree not available through ordinary reference service" (see brochure illustration).

Reactions to the programs of public libraries have been mixed. Many users and librarians from other organizations ask why it is necessary to have a fee-based information service in a free public library. The best answer may be the data that Minneapolis Public Library's Inform includes in one of its brochures (see brochure illustration).

The specific advantages that Inform offers to the library user have been cited as convenience, confidentiality, and flexibility. Visits are made to the customer's office to explain the service, discuss needs, or deliver information. The name of the client is kept strictly confidential. The Inform staff can, therefore, gather data for a client that wishes to keep its interest in a subject unknown. Every attempt is made to provide information in the format that is specified by the customer rather than the format in which it may be readily available.

The Denver Public Library is one of several libraries that experimented with fee-based information services in the mid-1970s, but dropped the program because of user resistance. Patrons refused to pay for staff time spent performing on-line

*INFORM-ation is decision making power

searches, the principal fee-based activity. A limited service in the areas of energy and environment has been reinstituted, aimed primarily at federal agencies in the community. For a fee of $10 per half hour, on-line and manual searches are provided to contract clients. In other areas, referrals are made to the Colorado State Library, which provides free on-line services. No alternatives for other services are offered.

Denver Public Library has been considering the reinstatement of on-line search services, with only the computer costs charged to the patron. Survey findings indicate five other fee-based information services that offer on-line search services in the Denver area alone, and none of the survey respondents note competition from the Denver Public Library or state libraries.

Even older than Denver's program is the John Crerar Library of the Illinois Institute of Technology in Chicago, an entire library serving only users who pay a fee for services. Academic libraries that have offered extensive fee-based information services include Georgia Institute of Technology (The Information Exchange Center, Atlanta), Southern Methodist University (Industrial Information Services, Dallas), University of Colorado (Colorado Technical Reference Center, Boulder), Rice University (Regional Information and Community Exchange, Houston), University of Wisconsin (Information Services Division, Madi-

INFORM is a nonprofit research service of the Minneapolis Public Library and Information Center providing you with business information:

- Industry overviews
- Competitor profiles
- Market studies
- Demographics
- Management strategies
- Biographical sketches
- And more......

In addition to specialized projects, INFORM offers a "current awareness" service that provides topical information on a scheduled basis.

Our information specialists have a professional, creative approach to problem solving. Top quality research is ensured through the utilization of diverse resources:

- Computerized data bases
- Trade associations
- Government publications
- Business journals, newspapers and magazines
- University collections
- Experts in the field

Because a successful project depends on transforming client questions into relevant answers, our end product is tailored to meet your unique information needs within your time demands.

Join such clients as manufacturers, consultants, market researchers, advertising agents, and sales representatives by calling INFORM for a free consultation. Fees are negotiated on a project basis. All transactions are confidential.

INFORM

Minneapolis Public Library & Information Center
300 Nicollet Mall
Minneapolis, MN 55401
(612)372-6636

son), and MIT Computerized Literature Search Service (formerly NASIC).

The fee-based information services have developed techniques that libraries may adopt more widely in the future. Their emphasis on information as a commodity with monetary value and their need to satisfy clients with cost-effective service have made them very conscious of the costs of accessing information and alert to alternative ways of gathering it.

One of the most widely used information-gathering and validating techniques employed by information services is telephone contacts with experts in a field. Timely data can be obtained at a very low price, especially by those firms that have special long-distance telephone service, something reference librarians may not have.

On-line searching is also widely used, not just because a client is paying for the service, but because information specialists generally accept the conclusions of studies that have evaluated the cost-effectiveness of on-line versus manual searching—on-line searching is generally more effective and less costly per citation than manual searching. On-line searching is still considered an exotic, high-cost service in most libraries because detailed cost studies are seldom undertaken. If all labor, library materials, space, and overhead costs were to be considered, the average in-depth reference question would probably cost as much as an on-line search. The widespread use of on-line searching by fee-based information services may influence libraries to use this tool more extensively.[11]

Marketing techniques are also being utilized by the more sophisticated fee-based information services. The most obvious are promotion techniques such as direct mail, Yellow Pages listings and advertisements, and promotional brochures. Even more important are the less visible market research techniques to determine market needs and wants. It is not enough to have a fine product or service; it must also be presented in a manner that reflects the attitudes of prospective clients. However, few libraries undertake market research, in the form of public opinion sampling, on a broad state or community basis.

A more subtle way in which fee-based information services may influence libraries is in their emphasis on an information-needs-of-users orientation rather than a books-and-journals orientation. Information is sought out wherever it is and by whatever techniques are appropriate and effective. This attitude has already pervaded much of special librarianship. Herbert White, past president of the Special Libraries Association, said as long ago as 1966: "The special library is that type of library which puts the needs of the user and the service requirements of meeting those needs above the principle of maintaining library service in accordance with any particular established traditions and techniques. Further, this service must be performed on the terms needed by the user, whether or not they conform to the library's own traditional pattern of operation."[12]

Special libraries have not necessarily embraced the fee-based information service industry, however. Inform polled some of the special librarians in their area and were told in many cases that these people had no trouble finding what their users wanted. The problem, of course, is available time. Corporate demands fluctuate; staff sizes stay relatively stable. The public library cannot normally accommodate an urgent request for special research even though the client's business may be at stake, because the library must necessarily be concerned with satisfying the cultural and recreational needs of an entire community.

Robert Taylor, dean of Syracuse University School of Information Studies, expressed the view that the library profession "must cut its umbilical cord to the library.... [It] is too important a profession to be tied to the fate of a single institution."[13] Taylor's school places over one-third of its graduates in fee-based information services rather than in libraries. Among the courses taught at Syracuse is marketing, a subject not common in the programs of other library science institutions.

Some schools of library and information sciences are adjusting their curricula. It is not clear whether the increasing emphasis on marketing, computer searching and applications, and the like will provide librarians with career alternatives or whether it will reshape the nature of libraries. In the opinion of the authors, the large majority of all persons completing the M.L.S. will continue to go into libraries at least during the 1980s. Not all of these will be imbued with enthusiasm for marketing and the use of computers, but many will be influenced. As these people rise to positions of leadership, the libraries will begin to reflect their perspective.

There has also been a great deal of activity by library schools to change their names. The most popular new name is "Graduate School of Library and Information Science" (see Preliminary List of Schools), but prospective students and employees have to examine the curricula carefully before concluding which institutions will best prepare people for careers that require marketing, computer searching, and other skills not common to·traditional library work.

A Preliminary List of Schools and Departments with a Concern for Information

University of California, Berkeley
Graduate School of Business Administration
School of Library and Information Studies

University of California, Los Angeles
Graduate School of Library and Information Science
Graduate School of Management

Carnegie Mellon University
Graduate School of Industrial Administration

Case Western Reserve University
School of Library Science

University of Chicago
Graduate Library School

Drexel University
School of Library and Information Science

Georgia Institute of Technology
School of Information and Computer Science

Harvard University
Master of Information Science Program

University of Maryland
College of Library and Information Services

Massachusetts Institute of Technology
Sloan School of Management

Michigan State University
Department of Communication

University of Minnesota
School of Business Administration

New York University
Graduate School of Business Administration

Ohio State University
Department of Computer and Information Science

University of Pennsylvania
Wharton School of Business

University of Pittsburgh
Graduate School of Library and Information Sciences

University of Southern California
Annenberg School of Communications

Stanford University
Graduate School of Business
Institute for Communication Research

Syracuse University
School of Information Studies

University of Texas
Graduate School of Business
Graduate School of Library Science

University of Washington
School of Communications

Reprint permission from Associated Information Managers. Resource Kit: "So You Want to Become an Information Manager." Preconference Seminar, NICE III, Washington, D.C., April 29, 1979.

It should not be assumed that the M.L.S. is the most appropriate degree for a person who wishes to become a principal in a fee-based information service. A number of people associated with the largest organizations in the field have degrees in journalism, business, or specialized disciplines. (Table 7 shows the background and training of principals of information services that were surveyed.) Many of their employees have subject degrees only. At this point, it seems doubtful that the traditional requirement of an M.L.S. to be appointed to a professional library position will be matched by the fee-based information services. Well-trained librarians will be in an excellent position to gain jobs in fee-based information services, but their advancement will depend on assertiveness, managerial skills, and other attributes to an even greater degree than has been the case with librarianship.

BASIC QUESTIONS AND ANSWERS

Q. Do fee-based information services exist in the public library?
A. Yes, in Cleveland, Dallas, Denver, Minneapolis, and Tulsa.
Q. What is their purpose?
A. According to Inform, the nonprofit research service of the Minneapolis Public Library, it is to "provide the user with access to library resources and professional skills to a degree not available through ordinary reference service."
Q. What other libraries offer fee-based services?
A. Academic libraries such as Georgia Institute of Technology and Southern Methodist University (Texas).

NOTES

1. "IIA Urges User Fees for Libraries in NCLIS Testimony," *American Libraries* 4 (June 1973): 335.
2. Fay Blake and Edith Perlmutter, "Libraries in the Marketplace," *Library Journal* 99 (January 15, 1974): 109.
3. Ibid., p. 108.
4. Richard De Gennaro, "Pay Libraries and User Charges," *Library Journal* 100 (February 15, 1975): 363.
5. Ibid., p. 364.
6. Ibid.
7. Ibid., p. 366.
8. Ibid., p. 367.
9. Barbara Whyte Felicetti, "Information for Fee and Information for Free: The Information Broker and the Public Librarian," *Public Library Quarterly* 1 (Spring 1979): 18.

TABLE 7 TRAINING AND BACKGROUND OF PRINCIPALS OF INFORMATION SERVICES

Degree	Large	Medium	Small	Free-lance	Non-profit	Canadian	Internal Services	Total
M.L.S.	—	6	14	23*	15	6	1	65
M.B.A.	2	1	6*	2	—	—	—	11
Journalism	2	1	—	1	—	1	—	5
L.L.B.	1	—	—	—	1	—	—	2
Library Experience	—	3	2	7	3	—	—	15
Other Work Experience	—	1	5	9	1	—	—	16
Advanced Degrees	—	3	3	4	2	—	—	12
Subject Degrees	—	—	—	2	1	—	1	4
On-Job Training	—	1	1	—	1	—	1	4
On-line Training	—	—	—	1	2	1	—	4

*Indicates one respondent has only partial degree.

Note: 37 principals of those surveyed indicated more than one degree or background; one Canadian nonprofit organization was included in the "nonprofit" category.

10. Solena V. Bryant, "The Information Industry and the Library—Competition or Cooperation?" address given at LACUNY Institute, April 16, 1979.
11. Dennis R. Elchesen, "Cost-Effectiveness Comparison of Manual and On-Line Retrospective Bibliographic Searching," *Journal of the American Society for Information Science,* March 1978, pp. 56–66.
12. Herbert S. White, "Special Librarianship—The Special One Is the Customer," *Minnesota Libraries* 16 (December 1966): 339–346.
13. "Information Entrepreneurs Stake Claims at LACUNY," *Library Journal* 104 (June 1, 1979): 1199.

11

WHAT HAPPENS NEXT?

The 1980s began with at least 100 active fee-based information services in the United States and Canada. There is no question that these services, and the information industry as a whole, will experience dramatic growth throughout the decade. That does not mean, of course, that all sectors of the industry will do well or that all who have already entered the field will survive. At least 21 information services went out of business during 1978 and 1979.

Among the comments from those who failed in 1979 was the statement that it was difficult to get marketing, billing, and bookkeeping aspects together—a common problem in new small businesses. Another found out—too late—that several government agencies performed the same services for nothing.

To a considerable extent, the industry has been built on its clients' lack of knowledge about alternative sources of information, including free or low-cost sources at government agencies and libraries.

One successful information service head said that "clients' standards are low due to ignorance—that's why we're in business." Another said that "it's reasonable to expect that clients will begin to investigate options when they begin to spend significant amounts of money."

The industry is not only vulnerable to a possible increase in client sophistication, but also to changes in technology. This is especially true of the segment that relies heavily on revenue from on-line searching. As low-cost terminals become widely available and searching strategies are simplified, more and more users will begin to do their own searching. Terminals with printers are now available for as little as $600. A Virginia-based information utility, called The Source, was delivering hundreds of databases to over 4,000 individual and small business users in late 1979, at prices as low as $2.75 per hour.

One of the future technologies that may impact on the information services is Teletext—a telephone-television system for information access from the home or office. Teletext piggybacks digital information on the regular television broadcast signal. The first U.S. consumer test of Teletext will be conducted by WETA/TV in Washington, D.C., in 1981. A closely related technology already beyond the initial test stage is Viewdata, developed as Prestel in the U.K. It is similar to Teletext, but it relies on transmission of the signal through telephone lines.

Viewdata was developed by the British Post Office, which also operates the telephone system in Great Britain. In operation, it has three components: the user with his or her television in the home or office, the post office, which provides the telephone line that transmits information and the computer that runs it, and the information providers who supply the actual text. The text itself is seen as a 24-line, 960-character page in up to seven colors. Logos and diagrams made up of blocks of color can also be displayed. Once the text is displayed, it can be read like the pages of a book and the pages changed at will. The modified television set has a small remote control keypad, which looks like a portable calculator. One punches in the individual user number and the system is ready to go.

Since a user proceeds by operating a 0–9 numerical keyboard and selects from a displayed choice until he or she receives the desired "information" page, no training is required. The first thing the user sees is the main contents page, which itemizes what information is available and directs the user to the subindexes covering individual sections. From the subindexes selected, the user is directed to the exact pages of information.

In Great Britain, several leading newspapers and newswire services have already signed up to provide the news, and a British publisher has begun to enter the contents of an entire encyclopedia. Initially, the British system has 250,000 pages available, but the next expansion will make one million pages available. The cost of modifying the television set is approximately $50, and there is a service charge of approximately $.01 per page for connect time to the computer. The information providers may charge up to $.04 per page. They must rent an editing terminal for data entry at a cost of $800 per year and pay a computer access fee of $500 plus $2 per page.

The forecast in Britain is four million users by 1985, which may be high; a slower growth rate than forecast may be attributable to a lack of marketing since the developing body is a government agency. It is worthy of note that the experience of American database and computer system developers has been that the home market responds much more slowly than the business community except in the case of entertainment products. If that is the case in all countries, the competing French system (Antiope), which is more highly subsidized, may establish a firmer foothold at an earlier date. Antiope was jointly developed by TDF (French Television Broadcasting Corporation) and the government agency DGT (Direction Generale des Telecommunication). The two have created a U.S. subsidiary called AVS, Inc. to market the system.

Computer networks may also impact on information services. EURONET, the computer network serving the countries of Western Europe, has established a Direct Information Access Network (DIANE) to serve as a "common market of information." The system has host computers in a number of locations to facilitate document delivery. The hosts serve as liaisons between the users and the document-fulfillment centers. A typical scenario might be:

> User identifies, on a terminal, reference citations desired and enters a print-order command at the end of the search.
>
> User, if he or she wishes, specifies the document-fulfillment center.
>
> Host computer stores request as a full bibliographic record in a "parking" file.
>
> User may alter request if he or she subsequently locates another reference.
>
> Host computer prints requests or order forms and distributes them to the appropriate fulfillment center. Or, alternately, the document-fulfillment center could, with its own terminal and printer, interrogate the host computer's parking file, and extract and print the orders directed to it.

The information providers could be publishers, database producers, government agencies, professional organizations, libraries, or information services. The fulfillment centers might be libraries or information services.

The future appears brightest for those who have an information product of some type to enter into a new electronic information system such as DIANE because once they have created a database, it can be used again and again, with a royalty to be paid on each use if the database creator so stipulates. The fulfillment centers, on the other hand, would only be able to charge for their labor and would have to expend it each time information was used. High-volume users, such as businesses, might choose to obtain terminals and become their own fulfillment centers.

The new technologies may lessen the importance of those who merely identify and deliver information, but they will not reduce the need for other types of intermediaries. As a wider range of information becomes available to the end users, especially information prepared by persons in other disciplines who use different methodologies and vocabularies, there will be more need for validation, interpretation, and evaluation. Information consulting may, therefore, become one of the next areas of emphasis for the information services. Consulting is already an important activity in the United States, with over 85,000 professionals engaged full time.

Some of the largest information services have already discovered that consulting services and specialized publication programs are more profitable than computer searching and quick-reference service. Many no longer accept simple reference questions except from retainer clients. Few of the firms with more than 20 employees wish to undertake projects that will result in a billing of less than $200.

The Illinois Institute of Technology Research Institute (IITRI) is an example of a large database searching service that is beginning to emphasize the design of databases and in-house information systems. Documentation Associates produces the United States Contract Awards (USCA) database, which is marketed through the SDC Orbit service. FIND/SVP and Washington Researchers have launched major publication programs and the Franklin Research Center has opted to bid on federal contracts for the establishment and operation of clearinghouses, which involve publishing, and the operation of large telephone banks, which give out standard information to thousands of callers.

The American pattern resembles that of the British, as reported by Christine Birks, who concluded in her study of the British marketplace:

> Research and advisory services have a brighter future [than searching and document delivery]. Several respondents intended to move up and market away from basic information work into analysis, evaluation, research, and consultancy.[1]

The impact of the new technologies may not be felt for five years or more. It appears that there will continue to be a great short-term demand for document delivery, especially directed to small firms and free-lancers. A large number of these requests may come from firms that have the ability to locate the information themselves, but find it more cost-effective to turn to an organization or individual who can perform the work at lower cost.

The trend over the first half of the 1980s may, therefore, be one of a very limited number of large information services emphasizing research and publication and a large number of very small services continuing to offer low-cost bibliographic searching and document delivery services. The large firms will continue to be concentrated in the major metropolitan areas and will remain national in their client base, while the small organizations and free-lancers will become even more widespread geographically, especially in the smaller metropolitan areas. Some of the medium-sized businesses may be absorbed by the large information services or they will develop specialities they can market nationally to special groups and to the larger information services. Specialization by industry is one possibility, especially in the areas of chemicals, food, and health care. It is very likely that large companies already in the publishing and database sectors of the information industry will launch specialized information services. McGraw-Hill, Dun and Bradstreet, 3M, General Electric, and Chase Manhattan Bank have already established marketing and information services.

The heavy dependence of many information services on large corporations as their principal source of business raises the question of how soon the special libraries in those client companies will begin to take on some of the functions of the information services. Most of these libraries have several professionals and substantial in-house collections. A majority have installed terminals for database searching. They are potentially capable of providing all the services that a fee-based information service provides except for anonymous third-party surveys of an industry. The number of positions in special libraries is declining rather than increasing, suggesting that any development of in-house information service capabilities is highly selective.[2]

The information needs of any organization will fluctuate, so it is not possible to have just the right amount of in-house staff to respond promptly to every need as it arises. Companies that provide word-processing services have learned that their best customers are often those who have in-house word-processing equipment, but whose workload periodically exceeds their capacity. These clients understand the procedures and costs involved and are able to clearly articulate the specifications for a project. Many special librarians are still reluctant to retain outside information services, possibly because they regard them as competition rather than as a supplement to the in-house activities. Effective marketing by fee-based information services may change these attitudes and create a reliable market for those firms that can adjust to fluctuating demand from clients with in-house capabilities. Since being the extra arms and legs for a company's special library is not a very profitable information service activity, that service is likely to be performed by the smaller and newer information firms in the field.

There has been much speculation that special libraries in large corporations will begin to offer information services to outside clients. This is apparently based on a trend of businesses to have libraries "charge back" the costs of their services to the units of the company that use them. As this often reduces demand on the library, at least temporarily, the library looks outside for clients who can provide incremental income. There is no evidence that any of these special libraries have actively promoted their services or have made significant amounts of money.

Most public and academic libraries decline to undertake time-consuming literature searches, bibliographies, report writing, translation, or other tasks for which they are not adequately staffed. Some refer these requests to fee-based information services, although a few libraries will perform them for a fee. Historically, librarians have been extremely reluctant to charge for services, out of both a conviction that library service should be free and a fear that to set fees might threaten the whole concept of the "free library."

Among the few public libraries that have established fee-based services are those in Cleveland, Dallas, Denver, and Minneapolis. The clients are almost exclusively corporations and government agencies. The volume of none of them is equal to any of the medium-sized or larger commercial information services. Predictions that public libraries will begin large-scale revenue-producing operations do not appear to have a factual foundation at this time. It is more probable that the libraries will place catalogs of their holdings and the community information that many of them now compile into Teletext systems or computer systems similar to DIANE.

There is a history of fee-based on-line literature searching in academic libraries. The fees usually recover only the computer and telecommunications costs. The searching is generally done for faculty and graduate students—on most campuses the primary users have been those with research grants to which the costs could be charged. In the future, when searching for undergraduates becomes more common, academic libraries may begin to undertake free on-line searching or to provide free terminals for their own patrons' use. This will be easier for academic libraries than for public libraries because the academic clienteles are much smaller and the per capita appropriations much higher. Academic libraries already limit some of their services by restrictive rules or policies rather than by levying fees.

The traditional library philosophy of free service may change, but it will take some time. By the time that occurs, the ownership of terminals by end users could be widespread. Rather than performing searches, the libraries are more likely to serve in an advisory capacity to those who need assistance in simple interpretation of what they have retrieved. Some of the searching systems being designed have "help" messages from time to time. The system will instruct the user that for assistance he or she can contact a reference librarian at the local library through the system. The librarian will be able to display the same information as the user to render assistance. The amount and type of free assistance may have to be limited to that which library patrons now receive in person because the budgets of libraries will place constraints on a major expansion of service. A few libraries may set fees for services provided to remote users. Again, the commercial services may play a supplementary role for those willing to pay for expanded service not available from libraries.

There is considerable evidence of cooperative activity among several large and medium-sized fee-based information services.

FIND/SVP, for example, has arrangements with other firms such as Packaged Facts, Environment Information Center, and Management Contents, and is able to offer a wider range of products and services as a result. The smaller companies benefit from the strong marketing unit that FIND/SVP has developed. This trend will grow as more of the medium-sized information services specialize. In 1980 two bibliographic database vendors, Lockheed and SDC, were providing an "electronic mailbox" for those searching on the terminals to place orders with document-delivery services such as INFORMATION ON DEMAND of Berkeley, California. As of June 1980, there were more than 30 DIALORDER suppliers—nearly double the number when the service was introduced. Of these, 10 are fee-based information services, four of which signed on as suppliers at the onset of the service.

> Carolina Library Services (Chapel Hill, N.C.)
> Colorado Technical Reference Center (Boulder, Colo.)
> Data-Search (Pittsboro, N.C.)
> DataQuest International, Inc. (Chicago, Ill.)
> FIND/SVP (N.Y.C.)
> Freelance Research Service (Houston, Tex.)
> INFO-SEARCH (Bloomfield Hill, Mich.)
> INFORMATION ON DEMAND (Berkeley, Calif.)
> Information Specialists (Cleveland Heights, Ohio)
> Information Store (San Francisco, Calif.)

Future trends indicate increasing participation of fee-based information services in "electronic mailbox" systems such as Lockheed's DIALORDER or SDC's Electronic Maildrop Service. Sue Rugge of INFORMATION ON DEMAND reported at the May 1980 NICE conference that DIALORDER has had a major impact on her document retrieval service. She stated that large segments of the marketplace have been exposed to commercial document retrieval services via electronic mail systems and that credibility and recognition of companies such as hers have increased greatly since the inception of such systems.

International cooperation is also increasing. Documentation Associates has entered into an agreement with Sorbil, based in Paris, for an exchange of document retrieval support. A number of other information service companies have also concluded international agreements.

While significant, the cooperative agreements will not

strengthen the firms with too limited a concept of the industry. The development of a new pattern of information service resembles that of the manufacturing sector. The database or information producers resemble the manufacturers; the information retrieval services resemble the distributors; and the information brokers, or those who sell the services, are the retailers. It is the retailing sector that faces the most uncertain future in the information industry, as is true in much of the manufacturing sector.

If an information broker is someone who on demand seeks to answer questions using all available sources and who is in business for a profit, the future is most uncertain because technology will bring many end users the means to do that for themselves. There is a much brighter future for those who describe their information services as individuals or organizations that solve information problems. Part of many information problems is the determination of the questions. In our complex society, one often cannot formulate the questions without expert advice.

The concept of information as a commodity is becoming widely accepted in our information-dependent society. Producers of information, especially those who can deliver it in machine-readable form, can expect both an increase in demand and a greater willingness to pay for information. Those who facilitate the distribution of information by providing telecommunications, computing facilities, or software will also experience considerable growth. Those who are able to "repackage" information quickly and economically in the form wanted by the user should be particularly successful because some will want highly specific information drawn from the entire body of data. Some will want it in printed form because they need numerous copies or lack Teletext or computer terminals.

Many of the information services were started by people who believed that there was a great unmet information need in small businesses. They may have been right, but there has apparently not been very much money spent to satisfy these needs; most of the revenue of the information services has come from other sectors. As the trend toward repackaging information in a number of ways continues, these services may actually begin to serve the market many of them first identified.

Those who have grown and prospered in the information service field have done so first by introducing the retainer concept to assure repeat business, second by vigorous marketing to provide volume, and third by developing products that can be sold again and again. The future addition of consulting, continuing education, or a number of other services is quite certain for it is only in this way that the fee-based information services can have predictable, steady sources of income.

In 1974, Andrew Garvin, president of FIND/SVP, estimated that the total private sector of the fee-based information services was a $5–$10 million per year industry and that within ten years it would grow to ten times that size.[3] Certainly, it has made great progress, for the industry is becoming more aware of itself as an industry—or at least as a distinguishable sector of the information industry. Top talent is being attracted to the field, and there is increasing awareness that effective marketing rather than improved information gathering is the most important challenge.

More of the future marketing should be marketing for the entire industry through a trade association. The Information Industry Association may serve this role if it is possible for the fee-based information service sector to obtain recognition as a significant, distinct subgroup within the larger industry group. This may not happen because the dollar volume of the information service sector is small when compared to the entire information industry.

Schools of library and information science can also contribute to the development of the field, as well as to changes in librarianship, by offering courses in the marketing of information services and in new technologies. A few are already beginning to do so, but the pace must be accelerated.

The field also needs to address other questions of common concern, such as the issues of legal liability of information services toward their customers, minimum standards for information specialists, and a professional code of ethics. These are typically the concerns of a maturing industry, and the fact that many persons in the field are thinking about them confirms the authors' opinion that the fee-based information service industry is on the road to maturity.

NOTES

1. C. I. Birks, *Information Services in the Market Place,* Research and Development Report, no. 5430 (London: The British Library, 1978), p. 50.
2. Elizabeth Fowler, "Careers: A Changing Field for Libraries," *New York Times,* February 7, 1979, p. D15.
3. Andrew Garvin, "Information-on-Demand Companies: Problems and Prospects," ASIS panel discussion, *Special Libraries* 67 (May/June 1976): 243.

Appendix I
SURVEY FORM

SURVEY OF FEE-BASED INFORMATION SERVICES

1. When was your business founded? _____

2. What are your business objectives? _____
_____
_____

3. What is your form of business organization?
   _____ a. corporation
   _____ b. partnership
   _____ c. sole proprietorship
   _____ d. other (explain) _____

4. What was your initial capitalization?
   _____ a. $1,000 or less
   _____ b. under $10,000
   _____ c. under $100,000
   _____ d. $100,000–$1,000,000
   _____ e. over $1,000,000

5. Do you employ personnel other than yourself? NO _____
   YES _____

6. If YES, how many full-time?
   _____ a. under 5
   _____ b. 5–10
   _____ c. 10–15

_____ d. 15–20
_____ e. 20–25
_____ f. 25–50
_____ g. over 50

7. What is the equivalent in full-time employees of your part-time staff? _____

8. What is the background of your research staff? What percentage have:
___% a. subject degree
___% b. library degree
___% c. library experience
___% d. other (explain) _____

9. What do you prefer to call yourself?
_____ a. information broker
_____ b. information specialist
_____ c. free-lance librarian
_____ d. information service
_____ e. library consultant
_____ f. other (explain) _____

10. What training helped you to prepare for your profession?
_____ a. MLS
_____ b. MBA
_____ c. other (explain) _____

11. What associations is your company active in?
_____ a. Information Industry Association
_____ b. American Society for Information Science
_____ c. Special Libraries Association
_____ d. American Library Association
_____ e. other (please name) _____

12. What types of services do you offer?
_____ a. analytical reports
_____ b. bibliographies
_____ c. consulting
_____ d. document delivery
_____ e. indexing
_____ f. information-on-demand
_____ g. manual searching
_____ h. market reports
_____ i. on-line searching
_____ j. publications (e.g., newsletters, directories, etc.)

_____ k. research
_____ l. SDI
_____ m. seminars, lectures, workshops
_____ n. translating
_____ o. other (describe) _____

13. What subjects are covered by your information service?
_____ a. Business
_____ b. Sci-Tech
_____ c. Health Sciences
_____ d. Humanities
_____ e. Social Sciences
_____ f. other (describe) _____

14. Who are your clients? Please indicate percentage of each:
_____% a. small business
_____% b. large corporations
_____% c. government agencies
_____% d. nonprofit organizations
_____% e. other (describe) _____

15. What is the proportion of your clients in the private sector?
_____ In the public sector? _____

16. What percentage of your clientele has dealt with you previously? (Please estimate) _____

17. What is the geographical distribution of your clientele? Please indicate percentage:
_____% a. community/local
_____% b. state
_____% c. regional
_____% d. national
_____% e. international

18. What activities are your clients engaged in? Please indicate percentage:
_____% a. marketing
_____% b. research & development
_____% c. administration
_____% d. other (explain) _____

19. Do your clients use the information service directly or do they go through an information intermediary (e.g., librarian or information specialist)? Please estimate percentage:
a. Direct: _____%   b. Intermediary: _____%

20. How do you obtain your business? Through:
        a. Advertising media:
_____   (1) telephone listings in white & yellow pages
_____   (2) yellow page advertising
_____   (3) radio ads
_____   (4) television ads
_____   (5) ads in professional journals
_____   (6) newspaper ads
_____ b. Direct Mail/Information Brochures
_____ c. Word-of-Mouth
_____ d. Conferences, Professional Institutes & Meetings
_____ e. Publications (e.g., newsletters)
_____ f. Products (e.g., market reports, directories)
_____ g. Seminars, Lectures, Workshops
_____ h. Sales Calls
_____ i. Editorial Coverage in Specialized Press
_____ j. Inducements
_____ k. Other (describe) _____

21. Which of the above is/are the most effective marketing tool(s) for your business? Indicate by letter(s): _____

22. Describe briefly a few typical projects with which you have been involved:

23. How many requests do you receive on an average per month? _____
Per year? _____

24. What sources do you utilize for answering requests? Please indicate percentage:
_____% a. in-house collections
_____% b. on-line databases
_____% c. nearby libraries
_____% d. telephoning experts
_____% e. other information services
        (1) For what types of information? _____
        _____
_____% f. other (explain) _____

25. Are there any restrictions placed on your company's use of libraries and other information services? NO _____ YES _____ If YES, explain: _____
_____

26. What is the proportion of requests received by:
    ___%__ a. telephone
    ___%__ b. mail
    ___%__ c. telex
    ___%__ d. in person
    Do you keep a record of this? NO _____ YES _____

27. What is your pricing strategy?
    _____ a. cost plus predetermined profit margin
    _____ b. rates set on basis of competitor's charges
    _____ c. negotiated fees
    _____ d. other (explain) _____

28. Why did you choose this pricing strategy? _____
    _____

29. What are your fees? _____

30. How do your clients pay for quick-information service?
    _____ a. in advance
    _____ b. by subscription/retainer
    _____ c. billed per job
    _____ d. other (explain) _____

31. How do your clients pay for research service?
    _____ a. in advance
    _____ b. by subscription/retainer
    _____ c. billed per job
    _____ d. other (explain) _____

32. Are there any free services (e.g., referral services)? NO _____
    YES _____

33. What percentage are your operating expenses of your
    billings? _____

34. Do you know of other information brokers who offer similar
    services? NO _____ YES _____
    If YES, please name: _____

35. Do you consider yourself in competition with any of them?
    NO _____ YES _____

36. If YES, is the competition regional, national, or interna-
    tional? _____

37. Does your information service assume legal liability for the
    accuracy of the information it provides? NO _____ YES _____
    Why is that? _____

38. How do you measure the effectiveness (quality and standards) of your operation?

39. What is the average turnaround time for completion of a job?

40. What new services do you plan in the near future?

41. What do you predict for your percentage rate of growth over the next five years?

42. What future do you see for information brokering?

Note: Is the attached description of your information service accurate? Please update if necessary and return with completed questionnaire.

Appendix 2
ASSOCIATIONS FOR SMALL BUSINESSES, NASA CENTERS, PANEL DISCUSSIONS/WORKSHOPS

TRADE AND OTHER (U.S.)

American Federation of Small Business
407 S. Dearborn St.
Chicago, IL 60605
(312) 427-0207
Educational programs, meetings, publications (bimonthly newsletters, statistical reports), provides speakers.

Chamber of Commerce
Local organizations are often helpful for small businesses.

International Council for Small Business (ICSB)
(formerly National Council for Small Business Management Development [NCSBMD])
University of Wisconsin—Extension
929 N. Sixth St.
Milwaukee, WI 53203
(414) 224-1818

Seminars, management training programs, annual conferences, publications (*Journal of Small Business Management*), maintains speakers bureau.

National Federation of Independent Business (NFIB)
490 L'Enfant Plaza East, S.W.
Suite 3206
Washington, DC 20024
(202) 554-9000
150 W. 20 Ave.
San Mateo, CA 94403
(415) 341-7441
Lobbying organization (federal and state levels), publications and reports on small business issues, newsletter (*The Mandate*).

Small Business Administration (SBA)
Washington, DC 20416

Local and regional offices throughout the U.S.; meetings, seminars, counseling, publications.

Smaller Business Association of New England (SBANE)
69 Hickory Dr.
Waltham, MA 02154
(617) 890-9070

Meetings, continuing education programs, newsletter publications.

FOR WOMEN IN BUSINESS

American Business Women's Association (ABWA)
9100 Ward Pkwy.
P.O. Box 8728
Kansas City, MO 69114
(816) 361-6621

Local chapters throughout the U.S.; programs, annual meetings, scholarships, publications (*Women in Business*).

American Women's Economic Development Corporation
1270 Avenue of the Americas
New York, NY 10020
(212) 397-0880

Counseling programs.

Coalition of Women in National and International Business
1038 Carew Tower
Cincinnati, OH 45202

Lobbying organization formed by participants at the White House Conference on Small Business.

National Association of Women Business Owners (NAWBO)
(formerly Association of Women Business Owners)
2000 P St., NW
Suite 410
Washington, DC 20036
(202) 338-8966

Meetings, workshops and seminars, information clearinghouse, referral and reader services, government representation, publications, provides network for women business owners.

Women Entrepreneurs
c/o Armitage Design
18 Brattle St.
Cambridge, MA 02138
(617) 492-0999

Meetings, programs, publications, regional network for women entrepreneurs.

Women Library Workers (WLW)
P.O. Box 9052
Berkeley, CA 94709

National organization with regional chapters; meetings, publications (newsletter, SHARE directory), supports women library workers (e.g., labor and discrimination cases), provides network for women library workers and alternative librarians.

U.K. ASSOCIATIONS

Association of Independent Businesses
Europe House
World Trade Center
London E1 9AA

General Secretary: Brendon Donolan

Confederation of British Industries
21 Tothill St.
London SW1H 9LP

Head of Smaller Firms: David Wilkins

NASA INDUSTRIAL APPLICATION CENTERS

These centers were established to provide information services and NASA documents.

Aerospace Research Applications Center (ARAC)
Indiana University/Purdue University at Indianapolis
1201 E. 38 St.
Indianapolis, IN 46205
(317) 264-4644
Director: E. Guy Buck

Kerr Industrial Applications Center (KIAC)
Southeastern Oklahoma State University
Durant, OK 74701
(405) 924-6822
Director: Robert E. Oliver

Knowledge Availability Systems Center (KASC)
University of Pittsburgh
Pittsburgh, PA 15260
(412) 624-5211
Director: Paul A. Williams

Nasa Industrial Applications Center (NIAC)
(formerly Western Research Applications Center)
University of Southern California
Denney Research Bldg.
Los Angeles, CA 90007
(213) 743-6132
Director: R.G. King

New England Research Applications Center (NERAC)
The University of Connecticut
Storrs, CT 06268
(203) 486-4533
Director: Daniel U. Wilde

North Carolina Science and Technology Research Center
P.O. Box 12235
Research Triangle Park, NC 27709
(919)549-0671
Director: Peter J. Chenery

Technical Applications Center
University of New Mexico
Albuquerque, NM 87131
(505)277-3622
Director: Stanley A. Morain

PANEL DISCUSSIONS/ WORKSHOPS

For information concerning availability of cassette tapes and/or transcripts of these panels/workshops, contact sponsoring association.

American Society for Information Science Annual Meeting, Atlanta, 1974.
"Information-On-Demand Companies: Problems and Prospects."
Participants:
Andrew Garvin, FIND/SVP
Alice Warner, Warner-Eddison Associates
Annette Hirsch, Information Specialists

Information Industry Association Annual Meeting, New York City, 1975.
"On Demand Custom Query Services."
Participants:
Annette Hirsch, Information Specialists (chairperson)
Gary Fiebert, Information for Business
Andrew Garvin, FIND/SVP
Elizabeth Eddison, Warner-Eddison Associates
Peter Leigh-Bell, Opidan Sciences, Inc.

Syracuse University, School of Information Studies Workshop, Drumlins, 1976.
"Information Broker/Free Lance Librarian—New Careers—New Library Services."
Participants:
   Maxine Davis, Information Access (chairperson)
   Susan Klement, Information Resources
   Christopher Samuels, Information for Business
   Carol Vantine, Inform
(Transcription available Syracuse University Miscellaneous Studies #3, edited by Barbara B. Minor.)

Information Industry Association, National Information Conference and Exposition II, Washington, D.C., 1977.
"How Information Brokers Provide Expert Access to Problem-Solving Information."
Participants:
   Elizabeth Eddison, Warner-Eddison Associates (chairperson)
   Georgia Finnigan, Information Unlimited
   Maxine Davis, Information Access
   Christopher Samuals, Information for Business
   Hood Roberts, Roberts Information Service
   Kathleen Bingham, FIND/SVP
   Annette Hirsch, Information Specialists
   Gordon Monsen, Editec
   Matthew Velucci, Consultant

LACUNY Institute (Library Association of the City University of New York), New York City, 1979.
"Information Service Entrepreneurs and Fee-Based Information Services in Libraries."

Participants:
   John Creps, Engineering Index (moderator)
   Jean Davenport, Facts for a Fee
   Oscar Firschein, Dialib
   Andrew Garvin, FIND/SVP
   Joseph Scorza, Rutgers University Research Information Service
   Alice Warner, Warner-Eddison Associates

Pratt Institute, School of Continuing Education Seminars, New York City, 1979–80.
"Designing and Marketing Information Products and Services."
"Marketing and Improving Utilization of Information Services."
Workshop Leaders:
   James Sanders, InterAmerica (moderator)

Information Industry Association, National Information Conference and Exposition (NICE IV), Washington, D.C., May 1980.
"Do It Yourself Business Kit."
Participants:
   Barbara Felicetti, INFO/MOTION (chairperson)
   Ruth A. Dwyier, Dwyier Associates, Inc.
   Don Grigg, Apr/Advertising and Public Relations
   Kathleen Lander, Lander and Associates
"Marketing Information Management." (Pt. II: Marketing Information Services)
Participants:
   Lorig Maranjian, Arthur D. Little/Probe
   Martin S. White, Business International/Creative Strategies, Inc.

Appendix 3
DIRECTORY OF FEE-BASED INFORMATION SERVICES— UNITED STATES, CANADA, THE U.K.

UNITED STATES

ARIZONA
Information Associates Ltd.
P.O. Box 18399
Tucson, AZ 85731
(602) 886-7074
Key Individual: Susan Singer
Abstracting, statistical reports, industrial forecasts, competition profiles.

ARKANSAS
Kay W. Colton
P.O. Box 391
Gould, AR 71643

Manual and computer searching, organization and development of libraries, directories, indexing, technical writing, investigative reports, purchasing services.

CALIFORNIA
Acquire Information
605 Cowper St.
Palo Alto, CA 94301
(415) 326-3996
Key Individual: Myra Hodgson
Manual and computer searching, information consulting.

Note: The following states are not listed: Alabama, Alaska, Delaware, Indiana, Louisiana, Maine, Mississippi, Montana, Nebraska, North Dakota, South Carolina, South Dakota, West Virginia, and Wyoming. This directory is based on individual and company responses to the authors' survey.

*The asterisk preceding an entry denotes nonprofit organization.

After-Image
6855 Santa Monica Blvd. #402
Los Angeles, CA 90038
(213) 467-6033
Key Individual: Ellen B. Henderson
Stock photography and photo research.

*Biological Information Service
8505 Brunswick Ave.
Riverside, CA 92504
(714) 689-2133
Key Individual: Julie L. Moore
Current-awareness searches; inhouse databases on wildlife species, marine mammals, oceanic birds, and bats retrospective searches (1934–date) on wildlife.

Ruth E. Carsch, Consulting Information Specialist
1453 Rhode Island St.
San Francisco, CA 94107
(415) 647-1629

Library and information facility long-range planning and development, library and information facility status quo evaluation, organization of unique information bases, cultural organization planning and development; specializing in technical engineering, fine arts, and architecture.

Cibbarelli and Associates
1800 Main St., Suite 230
Huntington Beach, CA 92648
(714) 842-6121
Key Individual: Pamela Cibbarelli
Design and implementation of information retrieval systems for business and industry, development of customized thesauri, creation of computerized library catalogs, on-line bibliographic database searching, compilation of topical bibliographies.

Competitive Market Intelligence
1717 N. Highland Ave., Suite 701
Los Angeles, CA 90028
(213) 463-0531
Key Individuals: Vickie M. Wilson, Rose Mary Smiley
Office libraries, file indexing and cross referencing, business intelligence files and periodical clipping systems; specializing in petroleum and petroleum-related industries.

Computerized Literature Searching Service
Central Univ. Library C-075
University of California–San Diego
La Jolla, CA 92093
(714) 452-4789
Key Individual: Bill Maina
On-line bibliographic database searching.

Decision Information Services, Ltd.
399 Sherman Ave., Suite 8
Palo Alto, CA 94306
(415) 327-0569
Key Individual: Colin Mick
Design, implementation, and evaluation of information systems and services, information needs assessment, design of information packages and planning for information programs and campaigns; specializing in scientific and technical communication, public dissemination, and education programs.

The Diversified Finders
5457A Paramount 103
Long Beach, CA 90805
(213) 630-3903

Key Individual: Thomas McKinnon
Research, preparation of indexes, compilation of bibliographies.

Documentation Associates
1513 Sixth St.
Santa Monica, CA 90401
(213) 393-6009
Key Individual: Kathleen Biveens
Manual and computerized literature searches, document delivery, information management, thesaurus construction, indexing, abstracting, bibliographic database construction.

Geoscience Information Service
Box 225
Chico, CA 95927
(916) 345-8610
Key Individual: Joseph Crotts
Indexing and proofreading of books, dissertations, and short papers; topical research, current-awareness, and SDI.

Global Engineering Documentation Services, Inc.
3301 W. MacArthur Blvd., Box 5020
Santa Ana, CA 92704
(714) 540-9870; (213) 624-1216
Key Individuals: Jerome H. Lieblich, Varnet Lieblich
Literature searching, document delivery, consulting; preparation of technical manuals for Army, Navy, and Air Force; specializing in specifications and standards from trade and professional societies and military and federal specifications and standards.

Info-Mart
Box 2400
Santa Barbara, CA 93120

(805) 965-5555; (805) 965-0265
Key Individual: Fred L. Bellomy
Customized literature searches—manual and on-line, annotated bibliographies.

Information Connection
5107 Calle Asilo
Santa Barbara, CA 93111
(805) 967-0922
Key Individuals: Linda and David Phillips
Computerized bibliographic research, document retrieval, report writing, technical consulting.

Information on Demand
2511 Channing Way, Box 4536
Berkeley, CA 94704
(415) 841-1145
Key Individual: Sue Rugge
Literature searching (manual and computer), document delivery, indexing, translating, current awareness, research.

The Information Store
235 Montgomery St., Suite 800
San Francisco, CA 94104
(415) 421-9376
Key Individual: Georgia Finnigan
On-line and manual searching, document delivery, market research.

Inquiry Reference and Information Center
Box 1411
Richmond, CA 94801
(415) 237-9835
Key Individual: Jeanette Bell-Lambert
Research and library reference; specializing in women's studies, black studies, American literature, and world history.

April Gerlitz Kelcy
4650 Encinas Dr.
La Canada, CA 91011
(213) 790-0835
Legal information retrieval systems, law library planning and development, legal research, bibliography preparation.

Richard L. King
12614 E. Park St.
Cerritos, CA 90701
(213) 926-3955
Consulting, manual and computerized literature searching, indexing and cataloging of information resources, SDI; specializing in literature on noise pollution.

Library Information Services
1563 Trestle Glen Rd.
Oakland, CA 94610
(415) 444-1998
Key Individual: Judith Demeter
Planning and organizing special libraries, slide libraries, records management systems, and microfilm systems, bibliographies and retrospective literature searching; specializing in architecture, engineering, business, and economics.

Barbara M. Lindemann
550 S. Barrington Ave. #1–110
Los Angeles, CA 90049
(213) 472-0905
Key Individuals: Barbara Lindemann, Paul Lindemann, Martin Auerbach
Literature searching, document delivery.

Martha Ammidon Powers
2661 Virginia St.
Berkeley, CA 94709
(415) 849-2471

Library reference and research, bibliographies, cataloging and organizing collections.

Research Ventures
3050 College Ave.
Berkeley, CA 94705
(415) 654-4810
Key Individuals: Marda Woodbury, Barbara Nozik, Annette Osenga
Research, bibliographies, annotations, organizing and maintaining library collections, editing, and writing.

Dawn M. Saunders
116 35 St.
Manhattan Beach, CA 90266
(213) 545-6450
Consulting, designing and developing information retrieval systems, library space planning.

Savage Information Services
30000 Cachan Pl.
Rancho Palo Verdes, CA 90274
(213) 377-4086, 337-7204
Key Individual: Gretchen (Sue) Savage
Research, consulting, database searching, document delivery, library operation and maintenance.

Seek Information Service
570 W. Terrace Dr., Box 216
San Dimas, CA 91773
(714) 599-2132; (213) 966-1013
Key Individual: Myra T. Grenier
On-line searching, consulting.

Alyce N. Shepard
16204 Estella Ave.
Cerritos, CA 90701
(213) 924-2000
Consulting, cataloging and indexing, library reference, setting

up technical processing departments.

Solar Energy Information Services
18 Second Ave., Box 204
San Mateo, CA 94401
(415) 347-2640
Key Individual: Justin A. Bereny
Manual and computer searching, document delivery, SDI, analytical reports; specializing in solar energy information.

Taylor & Associates
681 Market St., Suite 924
San Francisco, CA 94105
(415) 543-0125
Key Individuals: Kathryn E. Taylor, Ursula A. Bernhart
Library consulting and planning, systems design, library filing services; specializing in law libraries.

Umbrella Associates
Box 3692
Glendale, CA 91201
(213) 797-0514
Key Individual: Judith A. Hoffberg
Art information, bibliographies, indexing and organizing art files, consulting, publications.

***Women's Educational Equity Communications Network**
Far West Laboratory for Educational Research and Development
1855 Folsom St.
San Francisco, CA 94103
(415) 565-3032
Key Individuals: Matilda Butler, Fran Hereth
On-line searching, document delivery; specializing in publications on women's educational equity.

Women's History Research Center
2325 Oak St.
Berkeley, CA 94708
(415) 548-1770
Key Individuals: Laura X, Carolyn Moskovitz, Elizabeth Snowden
Research and resources on women's history; microfilm library collection and various publications for sale.

World Trade Business Information Center
Golden Gate Univ.
536 Mission St.
San Francisco, CA 94105
(415) 442-7244
Key Individual: Jeanne Nichols Sullivan
Computerized literature searching, statistics compilation, market surveys; specializing in international trade and business, tariffs and tax laws, product information.

Barbara Wurf, Indexpert
3122 Cardiff Ave.
Los Angeles, CA 90034
(213) 837-1654
Abstracting and indexing, bibliographic research, book indexing.

COLORADO

***Colorado Technical Reference Center**
Univ. of Colorado
Norlin Library, Campus Box 184
Boulder, CO 80309
(303) 492-8774
Key Individuals: Lynne Foot, Gayl Gray
Manual and on-line bibliographic searching, document delivery, bibliographies, SDI.

Barbara Conroy
Box 502
Tabernash, CO 80478
(303) 726-5260
Consulting, publications, evaluating educational programs, developing and writing proposals; specializing in staff training and development.

Information Management Specialists
2010 E. 17 Ave.
Denver, CO 80206
(303) 388-1987
Key Individuals: Diane S. Trumbo, Jeanne C. Raudenbush, Donna Good
Research, document delivery, management consulting, systems design and maintenance; specializing in engineering and energy.

Information Professionals
800 Washington St. #209
Denver, CO 80203
(303) 837-1293
Key Individual: Rebecca J. Jackson
Literature searching, automated and manual indexing, design of information retrieval systems, library management.

The Information Retriever, Inc.
2036 Glencoe St.
Denver, CO 80207
(303) 355-2562
Key Individual: Mary Lederer
Manual and computer searching, bibliographies, document delivery.

Library Reports and Research Service, Inc. (LRRS)
1660 S. Albion, Suite 400
Denver, CO 80222
(303) 758-5003
Key Individual: Judith A. Houk
Computerized and manual information retrieval, technical writing, publishing.

Library Services
1600 Broadway, Suite 1510
Denver, CO 80202
(303) 861-1720
Key Individuals: Judith K. Mahrer, Cassandra L. Roberts
Organizing in-house collections for law libraries and small businesses, updating loose-leaf services, research.

Organization Plus
1330 Rosemary St.
Denver, CO 80220
(303) 321-0038
Key Individual: Stella McBride
Management consulting, records management systems, seminars.

TechSearch
1492 Ammons St.
Lakewood, CO 80215
(303) 238-3460
Key Individuals: Susan O. Gallanter, Elizabeth Porter
Manual and computerized literature searching, document delivery, current awareness; specializing in mining and energy.

FLORIDA

*****FSU Search**
Strozier Library, Sci-Tech Div.
Florida State Univ.
Tallahassee, FL 32306
(904) 644-5534, 644-3079
Key Individuals: Helen Mannings, Jim Myers
Computerized bibliographic database searching.

William L. Needham
Box 3236
Tallahassee, FL 32303
(904) 386-1969
Research, designing and implementing information resources and systems, program planning.

*****Text Information Processing Services (TIPS)**
Univ. of Florida Libraries
Library West
Gainesville, FL 32611
(904) 392-0361
Key Individual: Dolores C. Jenkins
Computerized bibliographic database searching.

HAWAII
Library Information Service
3669 Kawelolani Pl.
Honolulu, HI 96816
(808) 737-4836
Key Individuals: Nancy V. Hellekson, Fanny L. Lilly
Specialized research, manual and computer searching.

IDAHO
Information Consultants
120 Elm Ave.
Rexburg, ID 83440
(208) 356-9055
Key Individual: Gale D. Reeser
Literature searching, consulting.

ILLINOIS

*****Computer Search Center**
Illinois Institute of Technology Research Institute (IITRI)
10 W. 35 St.
Chicago, IL 60616
(312) 567-4341

Key Individuals: Peter B. Schipma, Gerald J. Yucuis, Rebecca Gonzalez
Manual and computer searching, document delivery, SDI, analytical reports, quick-answer research, software development.

Dataquest International, Inc.
John Hancock Center, Suite 36-14
875 N. Michigan Ave.
Chicago, IL 60611
(312) 951-5351
Key Individual: Darlynn B. Beene
Customized research, bibliographies, computerized literature searching, document delivery, computerized indexing, translating, records management.

Editec, Inc.
175 W. Jackson Blvd.
Chicago, IL 60604
(312) 427-6760
Key Individual: Elecia Kerr
Retrospective and current awareness computer and manual literature searching, document retrieval, indexing, thesaurus development.

Infocorp
5559 N. Elston Ave.
Chicago, IL 60630
(312) 763-8707
Key Individual: Leo Schlosberg
On-line bibliographic searching, computerized indexing, software development, microform retrieval equipment, management information systems, consulting.

Searchline
Box F
Lisle, IL 60532
(312) 964-0127
Key Individuals: Ronald Scheidelman and Khalida Scheidelman

Computerized and manual searching, consulting, translating, specializing in chemistry, engineering, biomedicine and environmental science with emphasis on new products, product liability, and health.

Bet Yoatz Library Services
6247 N. Francisco Ave.
Chicago, IL 60659
(312) 262-8959
Key Individual: Daniel D. Stuhlman
Consulting, information systems analysis, publishing; specializing in Judaica collections.

IOWA

***Rare-Earth Information Center (RIC)**
Energy and Mineral Resources Research Institute
Iowa State Univ.
Ames, IA 50011
(515) 294-2272
Key Individual: Karl A. Gschneidner
Research, analytical reports, market surveys, document delivery, publications; specializing in rare earth metals and metallurgical applications.

KANSAS

Marianne Griffin & Associates
2720 Stratford Rd.
Lawrence, KS 66044
(913) 843-1254
Key Individuals: Marianne Griffin, Lois Clark, Linda Bailey
Research, consulting, manual and on-line literature searches, document delivery, organization of in-house collections, market research, public relations, interlibrary loan training, networking, clearinghouse for specialists and consultants.

KENTUCKY

The Gatherfacts Group (formerly Haynes-Allen Associates)
2915 Frankfort Ave.
Louisville, KY 40206
(502) 896-2988
Key Individuals: Gene Haynes, Ruth Allen
Manual and computerized literature searches, document delivery, bibliographies, abstracting and indexing, current awareness, organization and maintenance of in-house collections.

MARYLAND

Bogart-Brociner Associates
47 Williams Dr.
Annapolis, MD 21401
(301) 261-2893, 267-8354
Key Individual: Betty Bogart
Computerized bibliographic database searching, document delivery, research, translating.

Clearstory
11100 Montgomery Rd.
Beltsville, MD 20705
(301) 937-6733
Key Individual: Judy Watts
Literature searching, document retrieval, information organization; areas of specialization include science and technology, business, manufacturing, marketing, and the arts (fine and culinary).

Dataflow Systems Inc.
7758 Wisconsin Ave.
Bethesda, MD 20014
(301) 654-9133
Key Individual: Bill Doudnikoff
Manual and computer searching
(own database), indexing, analytical reports, seminars.

Infoquest (a service of Capital Systems Group)
11301 Rockville Pike
Kensington, MD 20795
(301) 881-9400
Key Individual: Alix Levy
Computerized literature searching, document retrieval, research studies, government activity monitoring and reporting; specializing in information services to the federal government with emphasis on health sciences and communications technology.

Mark F. German
2315 Washington Ave.
Chevy Chase, MD 20015
(301) 588-6138
General research, bibliographies, document search and retrieval, copyright searches.

Tracor Jitco, Inc.
1776 E. Jefferson St.
Rockville, MD 20852
(301) 881-2305
Key Individual: Randall Huffman
Customized information retrieval, analysis, and organization; specializing in biomedical and health sciences.

*Volunteers in Technical Assistance (VITA)
3706 Rhode Island Ave.
Mount Rainier, MD 20882
(301) 277-7700
Key Individual: Henry Norman

On-line searching, document retrieval, consulting, publications; specializing in solving technical problems for organizations and individuals in developing countries (U.S. AID programs).

MASSACHUSETTS
*Computerized Literature Search Service
Massachusetts Institute of Technology (MIT) Libraries,
Rm. 14SM-48
77 Massachusetts Ave.
Cambridge, MA 02139
(617) 253-7746
Key Individuals: Mary E. Pensyl, Susan E. Woodford
Computerized bibliographic database searching (retrospective and SDI), available to non-MIT researchers.

Info/Motion
214 W. Mountain Rd.
Lenox, MA 01240
(413) 637-2156
Key Individual: Barbara Whyte Felicetti
Manual and computer literature research, document retrieval, consulting, cataloging, indexing, current awareness, SDI, reports, workshops, library organization; areas of specialization include business, government, employment of the handicapped, education, mental health, cinema, and demography.

Information Resources
11 Hale Ave.
Winthrop, MA 02152
(617) 846-8578

Key Individuals: Karen Luongo, Christina V. Murphy
Literature searching, document retrieval, consulting, research, bibliographies, indexing, analytical reports, publications.

Arthur D. Little/Probe
Decision Resources
Acorn Park #17
Cambridge, MA 02140
(617) 864-5770
Key Individual: Anne V. Quinn
Customized information research, manual and computer searching, indexing, analytical reports, current awareness and issue tracking, information audit, patent searching; specializing in physical, life, and environment sciences, business and economics, social sciences.

On Hand Advisory Service
8 Warwick Terr.
Marblehead, MA 01945
(617) 631-5379, 631-6807
Key Individuals: Sara Posner and Gerald Posner
Research, bibliographies, library organization, publications, direct-mail consultations.

*Present Futures
119 Mt. Auburn St.
Cambridge, MA 02138
(617) 492-8914
Key Individuals: Tina Dong, Frank Catanzaro
Online community development, "peopleware" indexing, computer conferencing, barter referral, feminist studies.

Warner-Eddison Associates, Inc.
186 Alewife Brook Pkwy.
Cambridge, MA 02138
(617) 661-8124

Key Individuals: Elizabeth Bole Eddison, Alice Sizer Warner
Manual and computer literature searching, indexing, records management systems, designing and organizing technical libraries and information centers, consulting, current awareness and alerting services, library maintenance.

MICHIGAN
Info-Search
1520 N. Woodward, Suite 110
Bloomfield Hills, MI 48013
(313) 642-5446
Key Individual: Gloria Donoher
Manual and computer searching, document retrieval, market research, current awareness, library organization, non-legal research; specializing in marketing and technical information for suppliers to the automotive industry.

*Science Book & Serial Exchange
525 Fourth Street
Ann Arbor, MI 48103
(313) 665-0537
Key Individual: Raymond L. Hough
Exchange of scientific and technical publications, out-of-print search service.

MINNESOTA
*Inform
Minneapolis Public Library & Information Center
300 Nicollet Mall
Minneapolis, MN 55401
(612) 372-6636
Key Individual: Maggie Hansen

Manual and computerized literature searching, document retrieval, bibliographies, current awareness; specializing in financial or marketing information, industry overviews, company profiles, demographics, economic indicators.

MISSOURI
Jan Cutsinger
3804 Opal Dr.
St. Charles, MO 63301
(314) 447-2625
Research, bibliographies, indexing, records management consulting, library organization, genealogical research.

Information Resource Consultants
11920 Hargrove
St. Louis, MO 63131
(314) 822-3762, 524-2842
Key Individual: Suzanne Gill
Designing information retrieval systems, organizing information centers, staff development training.

NEVADA
Deborah Hunt: Consulting Information Specialist
1920 Bonneville Ave.
Reno, NV 89503
(702) 747-3693
On-line bibliographic searching, research, library organization, staff training.

NEW JERSEY
Fact Finders
900 Glenview Rd.
Ridgewood, NJ 07450
(201) 444-9191

Key Individuals: Norma Levy, R. Garoogian
Literature searching, document retrieval, research, collection evaluation, library systems development and maintenance.

Information Plus
15 Vose Ave.
South Orange, NJ 07079
(201) 763-1773
Key Individual: Catherine Sullivan
Research, bibliographies, consulting, organization of information resources; specializing in marketing information.

MBP/Information Research
38 W. Main St.
Bergenfield, NJ 07621
(201) 385-8225
Key Individual: Pierre Papazian
Manual and computer searching, document delivery, SDI, research, analytical reports, bibliographies, indexing; specializing in international relations, political history (Middle East), Soviet nationality problems, genetic diseases.

***Research Information Services**
Rutgers Univ./The State Univ. of New Jersey Libraries
College Ave. & Huntington Sts.
New Brunswick, NJ 08901
(201) 932-7685
Key Individual: Joseph C. Scorza
Manual and computerized literature searching; available only to the public, institutions, and businesses of New Jersey.

George F. Smith Library of the Health Sciences
College of Medicine & Dentistry of New Jersey

100 Bergen St.
Newark, NJ 07103
(201) 456-5318
Key Individual: Michael Brandli
Computerized bibliographic database searching, SDI, specializing in biomedicine, dentistry, and nursing.

TCR Service, Inc.
140 Sylvan Ave.
Englewood Cliffs, NJ 07632
(201) 461-7475; (212) 986-8117
Key Individuals: Irving Ruzan, Mary B. Sheehan
Manual and computer searching, reports, publications, vigilance or alert service; specializing in patent and trademark searching.

Unlisted Drugs/Pharmaco-Medical Documentation, Inc.
205 Main St.
Chatham, NJ 07928
(201) 635-9500
Key Individual: Boris R. Anzlowar
Manual and computerized literature searching, analytical reports, translating, indexing; specializing in biomedical, drug, and pharmaceutical information.

NEW MEXICO
*Access to Information, Inc.
1170B Camino Delora
Santa Fe, NM 87501
(505) 988-5095
Key Individual: Jerry Zollars
Manual and computerized literature research, document retrieval, consulting; specializing in legal and educational research and technical information retrieval systems.

*Bureau of Business and Economic Research
Institute for Applied Research Services
The Univ. of New Mexico
Albuquerque, NM 87131
(505) 277-2216
Key Individual: Betsie Kasner
Literature searching, document retrieval; specializing in business, economics, and management.

NEW YORK
Chase Manhattan Bank/The Information Center
One Chase Manhattan Plaza
New York, NY
(212) 522-8014
Key Individual: Roger G. Fohl
Manual and computerized literature searching, document retrieval, publications (*Biz-dex*).

*Engineering Societies Library
345 E. 47 St.
New York, NY 10017
(212) 644-7611
Key Individual: S. Kirk Cabeen
Literature searching, document retrieval, bibliographies, publications (*Engineering Index*); specializing in all fields of engineering.

Environment Information Center, Inc. (EIC)
292 Madison Ave.
New York, NY 10017
(212) 949-9494
Key Individuals: James G. Kollegger, Robert D. Howells, Karen J. Ziegler
Computerized on-line systems; abstracting, publications, microfiche library systems; specializing in energy and environmental databases.

Loren V. Fay
RD 3
Moravia, NY 13118
(315) 497-0607
Genealogical research, publications.

Find/SVP
The Information Clearing House, Inc.
500 Fifth Ave.
New York, NY 10036
(212) 354-2424
Key Individuals: Andrew P. Garvin, Kathleen S. Bingham
Manual and computerized literature searching, document retrieval, information-on-demand, market research, SDI, current awareness, publications; specializing in business information and health care.

Judith Finell Musicservices, Inc.
155 W. 68 St.
New York, NY 10023
(212) 580-4500
Research (music plagiarism cases), editing and writing, cataloging, counseling, program planning, publications; specializing in music, dance, opera, and the arts.

Dorothy M. Greninger
131 Durland Pl.
Watkins Glen, NY 14891
(607) 535-4524
Technical literature searching (manual and computer), technical writing and editing; specializing in food chemistry, analytical chemistry, environmental hazard assessment, nonferrous metals, household products, organic chemicals.

Jane Huang
Box 165
Delmar, NY 12054
(518) 439-6295
Manual and computerized literature searching, document retrieval, bibliographies, indexing, translating; specializing in medicine and business information.

*ILR: Access
Martin P. Catherwood Library
New York State School of Industrial and Labor Relations
Cornell Univ., Box 1000
Ithaca, NY 14853
(607) 256-2277
Key Individual: Gordon T. Law
Manual and computerized literature searching, document retrieval, bibliographies, research; specializing in industrial relations, collective bargaining, labor law, personnel management, labor market, labor force, human resources, an organizational behavior.

In-Fact
Box 151
Rensselaerville, NY 12147
(914) 797-5154
Key Individuals: Kate Storms and Ken Storms
Literature searching, bibliographies, consulting, editing, genealogical and legal research, records management, planning archives and library collections.

Information for Business
25 W. 39 St.
New York, NY 10018
(212) 840-1220
50 Church St.
Cambridge, MA 02138
(617) 876-7776

Key Individuals: James C. Burke, Christopher J. Samuals, Catherine A. Slade

Customized research, analytical reports; planning, developing and operating information centers, research centers, and records management facilities; specializing in business and industrial research.

Information Services
205 Highland Pkwy.
Rochester, NY 14620
(716) 271-7164
Key Individual: Sara McCain
Literature searching, bibliographies, research, indexing, translating, proposal writing, cataloging and classification, archival and manuscript management.

Information Services and Research
University Sta. Box 95
Syracuse, NY 13210
(315) 483-5479
Key Individual: Brian E. McLaughlin
Information resources organization and development, strategic planning, grantsmanship.

Information Yield
311 Stonecrest Dr.
Syracuse, NY 13214
(315) 445-0484
Key Individual: George L. Abbott
Customized bibliographies, information consulting, conference and workshop management; specializing in business management, reprographics, and audio-visual utilization.

Informatron
1401 Carroll St.
Brooklyn, NY 11213

(212) 493-6041
Key Individuals: Rose Coppola, Marguerita Roett
Literature searching, current awareness, consulting, developing information centers, records management.

Informedia
Box 1020
Pearl River, NY 10965
(914) 735-4342
Key Individual: Mary R. Sive
Manual and computerized literature searching, document delivery, SDI, analytical reports, indexing, publications, alerting service on current topics (energy, women's studies, ethnic studies, etc.).

McGraw-Hill Publishing Co./Marketing Information Center
1221 Ave. of the Americas
New York, NY 10020
(212) 997-3222
Key Individual: Shirley Keating
Literature searching, market research, analytical reports, current awareness, SDI.

Marshe Infoservices, Inc.
3099 Beltagh Ave.
Wantagh, NY 11793
(516) 627-3127, 826-3261
Key Individuals: Sherry Powell, Marilyn Stern
Literature searching, bibliographies, indexing and abstracting, business information, organizing collections.

*National Investment Library
80 Wall St.
New York, NY 10005
(212) 982-2000, (800) 221-5644
Key Individuals: Michael Barrett, Patrick Sherran

Manual searching, document retrieval, analytical reports, business and financial information.

Omniquest Inc.
Box 15
Chappaqua, NY 10514
(914) 238-9646
Key Individual: Vicki Mechner
Manual and computerized literature searching, document retrieval, bibliographies, research, analytical reports, publications (newsletter).

Packaged Facts, Inc.
274 Madison Ave.
New York, NY 10016
(212) 532-5533
Key Individuals: David A. Weiss, Joseph Castrovilla
Literature searching, market studies, historical research, trademark research, backdated clippings.

Research Reports
315 W. 78 St.
New York, NY 10024
(212) 595-6770
Key Individuals: Ann Novotny, Rosemary Eakins
Photo research, visual consulting, editorial research and fact finding, specialized bibliographies, interviewing, editing, and writing.

Jay D. Tebo
1101 Ford Rd.
Vestal, NY 13850
(607) 754-6922
Literature searching, document delivery, bibliographies, consulting, planning and organizing collections; specializing in business and engineering research.

Technical Library Service, Inc.
130 Fifth Ave.
New York, NY 10011
(212) 675-0718
Key Individual: Elaine Haas
Literature searching, bibliographies, translating, indexing and abstracting, purchasing services, developing library collections.

World Wide Information Services, Inc.
660 First Ave.
New York, NY 10016
(212) 679-7240
Key Individual: Richard W. Hubbell
Business/financial intelligence and market research, specialized commercial news service.

*World Trade Information Center
One World Trade Center, Suite 86001
New York, NY 10048
(212) 466-3064
Key Individuals: Gerald Lieberman, Rose E. Callahan
Manual and computerized literature searching, custom research, analytical reports.

NORTH CAROLINA

Carolina Library Services
137 E. Rosemary St.
Chapel Hill, NC 27514
(919) 929-4870
Key Individual: Eva Metzger
Online searching, document delivery, current awareness.

Data-Search
Box 635
Pittsboro, NC 27312
(919) 542-5114

Key Individual: Alan Metter
Manual and computerized literature searching, document delivery, research, current awareness, analytical reports.

OHIO
*Chemical Data Center, Inc.
3620 N. High St.
Columbus, OH 43214
(614) 261-7101
Key Individuals: Kenneth E. Jackson, Lucy E. Martin
Manual and computerized literature searching, SDI, document retrieval, bibliographies, technology summaries.

*Facts for a Fee
Cleveland Public Library
325 Superior Ave.
Cleveland, OH 44114
(216) 623-2999
Key Individual: Jean Davenport
Manual and computerized literature searching, document retrieval, bibliographies.

Information Specialists
2490 Lee Blvd.
Cleveland, OH 44118
(216) 321-7500
Key Individual: Annette M. Hirsch
Manual and computerized literature searching, document delivery, research, tracking services; specializing in market and product research.

*Mechanized Information Center (MIC)
The Ohio State Univ. Libraries
1858 Neil Ave. Mall
Columbus, OH 43210
(614) 422-3480
Key Individual: Bernard Bayer

Manual and computerized literature searching, bibliographies, SDI computerized indexing.

OKLAHOMA
*Info II
Tulsa City–County Library
400 Civic Center
Tulsa, OK 74103
(918) 581-5219
Key Individuals: Jane Colwin, Linda Hill
Manual and computerized searching, document retrieval, current awareness, statistical compilations.

OREGON
Northwest Information Enterprises
2383 N.W. 153
Beaverton, OR 97006
(503) 645-1832
Key Individual: Julie Kawabata
Manual and computerized literature searching, bibliographies, indexing, abstracting, organizing and maintaining collections, information management, editing.

PENNSYLVANIA
Herman Baron
Box 194
Moylan, PA 19065
(215) 565-0362
Consulting, indexing and editing, on-line searching, document delivery, bibliographies, production of directories, catalogs, and indexes, museum collections inventory, computer typesetting; specializing in library automation, financial management,

Oriental art, and organization of archival and museum collectibles.

*Franklin Research Center
Science Information Services Organization (SISO)
20 & Benjamin Franklin Pkwy.
Philadelphia, PA 19103
(215) 448-1464, 448-1227
Key Individual: Alec Peters
Manual and computerized literature searching, document delivery, SDI, analytical reports, translating, indexing; specializing in air pollution control, water pollution and water resources, solid waste management, metal organic chemistry.

Info/Consult
Box 204
Bala Cynwyd, PA 19004
(215) 667-3088, 667-0266
Key Individual: Gabrielle Revesz
Manual and computer searching; indexing and abstracting, patent and trademark searching, market research, bibliographies, analytical reports.

Infosense Consulting Services
Box 97
Narberth, PA 19072
(215) 386-1477
Key Individual: Shirley B. Thurston
Research, consulting—information organization (office systems, records management, micrographics, word processing), analytical reports.

Library Information and Research Service
1214 Bennington Ave.
Pittsburgh, PA 15217
(412) 682-6096, 661-1795

Key Individuals: Amy C. Lowenstein, Roxine M. Weinthal
Literature searching, research in medical information.

*Medical Documentation Service
College of Physicians
19 S. 22 St.
Philadelphia, PA 19103
(215) 563-1238
Key Individual: Alberta D. Berton
Manual and computer searching, SDI, document delivery, analytical reports, abstracting and indexing, translating, editing, and medical writing; specializing in biomedical and life sciences.

Posts' Information Service
4613 Larchwood Ave.
Philadelphia, PA 19143
(215) 748-2701
Key Individual: Joyce Post
Manual and computerized literature searching, bibliographies, indexing and index design, thesaurus development; specializing in television and motion pictures, communications and journalism, travel and geography, and nontechnical information.

Doris P. Shalley
General Sullivan Rd.
Washington Crossing, PA 18977
(215) 493-3521
Research, indexing, picture search, copy editing, manuscript analysis, consulting.

TEXAS
*Dallas Public Library/Custom Research Services
1954 Commerce St.
Dallas, TX 75201
(214) 748-9071

Key Individuals: Ralph M. Edwards, Jane Mann
Computerized bibliographic database searching.

Freelance Research Service
1006 Missouri
Houston, TX 77006
(713) 526-8058
Key Individual: Jennifer Reavis
Research, literature searching, document delivery, records management.

Library Management and Services
5914 Highland Hills Dr.
Austin, TX 78731
(514) 454-7229
Key Individual: Judith Helburn
Consulting, legal research, library management (cataloging systems, file services, etc.), publications (*Practical Law Books Review,* quarterly newsletter).

Regional Information and Communication Exchange
Fondren Library
Rice Univ.
Houston, TX 77001
(713) 528-3553
Key Individuals: Daniel T. Law, Tina Byrne
Manual and computerized bibliographic searching, document retrieval, translating; specializing in sci-tech and business information.

UTAH

Golden V. Adams, Jr.
961 W. 100 South
Provo, UT 84601
(801) 375-3872
Key Individuals: Golden Adams and Diane Adams

Genealogical research, consulting, record searching, compilations, publications, seminars.

Western Consultants
1663 S. 75 East
Bountiful, UT 84010
(801) 292-0041
Key Individual: Jay L. Bishop
Genealogical and historical research, paleography, translating, compilations.

VERMONT
Information Control(ICO)
86 Hazel St.
Rutland, VT 05701
(802) 775-0179
Key Individual: James S. Davidson
Reseach, public relations and problem-solving information services, organization of information, publications.

Vermont Information Processes (VIP)
23 Burnham Ave.
Rutland, VT 05701
(802) 773-2711 Ext. 266
Key Individual: Olga M. Compton
Manual and computerized literature searching, document retrieval, indexing and abstracting; specializing in energy and business information.

VIRGINIA
Atlantic Research Corporation
5390 Cherokee Ave.
Alexandria, VA 22314
(703) 642-4189
Key Individuals: Judith F. Kitchens, Ralph S. Valentine
Manual and computerized literature searching, document retrieval, analytical reports; spe-

cializing in environmental research and pollution technology (military projects).

InterAmerica Research Associates
Information Management Services
1555 Wilson Blvd., Suite 600
Rosslyn, VA 22209
(703) 522-0870
Clearinghouse design and development, database development and management, abstracting and indexing, inquiry and referral systems development and management, cataloging and library services, publications, computerized literature searching (in association with the National Clearinghouse for Bilingual Education).

Roberts Information Services
8505-G Merrifield Ave.
Fairfax, VA 22030
(703) 560-7883
Key Individual: Hood Roberts
Computer searching government document delivery, Freedom of Information Act inquiries.

WASHINGTON, D.C.
Facs Inc.
747 National Press Bldg.
Washington, DC 20045
(202) 347-8450
Key Individual: Arthur Lewis
Research, SDI, document delivery, subscription and filing services; specializing in government documents.

Information & Research International
The East Asia Research Institute
850 National Press Bldg.
Washington, DC 20045
(202) 638-5877

Key Individual: Thomas Hosuck Kang
Literature searching, research, consulting, document retrieval, indexing, and abstracting; specializing in East Asian, Chinese, Japanese, and Korean information.

Picture Research
6307 Bannockburn Dr.
Washington, DC 20034
(301) 229-6722
Key Individual: Grace E. Evans
Picture (stills, film footage) research, consulting.

Science Information Services
Pharmaceutical Manufacturers Association (PMA)
1155 M St., N.W.
Washington, DC 20005
(202) 296-2440
Key Individual: Patricia O'Brien
Manual and computerized literature searching, SDI, specializing in pharmaceutical information.

Patricia K. Smith
L'Enfant Plaza Sta., Box 23737
Washington, DC 20024
(703) 548-0041
Designing information systems; specializing in economics, energy, medicine, marine science, and congressional lobbying.

Washington Representative Services
4040 N. Fairfax Dr. #110
Arlington, VA 22203
(703) 243-8912
Key Individual: Beverly Kooi
Manual searching, document delivery, analytical reports, facsimile service, abstracting; specializing in grant programs and government information.

Washington Researchers
910 17 St., N.W.
Washington, DC 20006
(202) 833-2330
Key Individuals: Matthew Lesko,
Leila Kight
Customized research, publications
(guides, directories), instruc-
tional seminars; in business,
government, corporate, industry, international business information, market research, and
corporate planning.

WISCONSIN
Badger Infosearch
P.O. Box 11943
Milwaukee, WI 53211
(414) 964-2377
Key Individual: Darlene E. Waterstreet
Research (legal and business), consulting, indexing, library organization, records management.

CANADA

ALBERTA
*****Alberta Research Council**
11315-87 Ave.
Edmonton, AB T6G 2C2
(403) 432-8059
Key Individuals: A. Fitzpatrick,
Mary Hart
Computerized literature searching, document delivery, SDI,
indexing, seminars, publications; serves all Alberta industries.

**Schick Information Systems,
Ltd. (SIS)**
10011 80 Ave.
Edmonton, AB T6E 1T4

(403) 432-7621
Key Individuals: Patricia Schick,
Moira Moore
Literature searching, bibliographies, information-on-demand,
consulting, designing and
maintaining information systems, records management,
computerized indexing.

BRITISH COLUMBIA
ISI Infosearch, Inc.
123-3755 W. Sixth Ave.
Vancouver, BC V6R 1T9
(604) 224-1168
Key Individual: Diana Broome
Computerized literature searching, document delivery, bibliographies, indexing, and abstracting.

ONTARIO
Canadatum
1124 Eglinton Ave. W., Suite 2
Toronto, ON M6C 2E2
(416) 783-1475
Key Individuals: Annette Snow-
don, Mary Jo Anderson
Research for public relations
firms, fact-checking, copy and
speech writing, picture research.

**Michael A. Dagg Associates/
Associés**
Box 9211
Ottawa, ON K1G 3T9
(613) 741-5274
Key Individual: Michael A. Dagg
Literature searching, research, re-
ports, indexing, bilingual trans-
lations; specializing in Cana-
dian government publications.

Information Resources
45 Inglewood Dr.
Toronto, ON M4T 1G9
(416) 486-0239
Key Individual: Susan Klement
Manual and computerized literature searching, document retrieval, bibliographies, current awareness, thesaurus construction, indexing and abstracting, report writing, workshops and seminars, consulting.

Micromedia Ltd.
144 Front St. West
Toronto, ON M5G 1J2
(416) 593-5211
Key Individual: Robert Gibson
Information on demand, computerized literature searching.

Dean Tudor
Library Arts
Ryerson Polytechnical Institution
50 Gould St.
Toronto, ON M5B 1E8
Bibliographic advice, indexing, reports, consulting.

THE U.K.

Capital Planning Information, Ltd.
2 Birling Rd.
Tunbridge, Scotland
(0892) 32906
and
12 Castle St.
Edinburgh, Scotland
(031) 226 4367
Key Individuals: Don Kennington, Brenda White
Consultancy and research, information management, training, and seminars, information on demand and document re-

trieval; specializing in planning, housing, and urban documentation fields.

European Community Investigation Services (ECI)
88-90 Grays Inn Rd.
London WC1Z 8AA
(01) 242 8088
Key Individual: Caroline Heller
Monitoring, research and analysis, consultancy, special reports, assistance on grant applications, contacts for lobbying; specializing in European Community affairs.

Financial Times/Business Information Service
Bracken House
10 Cannon St.
London EC4P 4BY
Key Individual: Philip Healy
(01) 248 8000
Consultancy, market research, on-line retrieval, press cuttings.

Focus on Information, Ltd.
186 Westcombe Hill
Blackheath, London SE3 7DH
(01) 628 6767 / (01) 852 6098
Key Individuals: George Bunce, Colin Godley, D. Nicholas, W.E. Duncan
Marketing research, monitoring services, bibliographies, consultancy (design and implementation of managerial information systems), technical library organization.

Geosystems
P.O. Box 1024
Westminster, London SW1
(01) 222 7305
Key Individual: Graham Lea
Consultancy, database design, indexing, on-line searching, docu-

ment delivery; specializing in geoscience, earth science, energy, and mining.

Information Research, Ltd.
Bond St. House
Clifford St.
London W1
(01) 491 7693
Desk research, market studies.

Irish Roots
12 Gerald Rd.
London SW1
(01) 730 2773
Key Individual: Lorna Rosbottom
Genealogical research.

London Researchers
Sussex Place, Regents Park
London NW1
(01) 723 3902
Key Individual: Nigel Oxbrow
Desk research, seminars, design and implementation of information centres for desk research.

The Marketing Shop
Hedges House
153/155 Regent St.
London W1R 7FD
(01) 439 8847
Key Individual: Carl Morris
Desk research, monitoring and statistical services, market studies, forecasting and analysis, marketing planning, and product development.

Metals Information Service
The Metals Society
1 Carlton House Terrace
London SW1
(01) 839 4071
Key Individual: John Baughan
Retrospective and current awareness on-line searching, abstracting and indexing, consultancy and training, document delivery, technical translations,

bibliographies, industry profiles, database production (METADEX, ABTICS, etc.).

Metra Consulting Group
Information Dept.
23 Lower Belgrave St.
London SW 1
(01) 730 0855
Key Individual: Thomas Landau
Consultancy for international organizations, government departments and industry; library and archival organization (Paris office).

NPM Information Services
New Product Management Group
Management House
Parker St.
London WC2B 5PT
(01) 404 5414
Key Individual: Dr. Gordan Wilkins
Desk research, on-line searching, patent information, market research, information audit, translating, seminars and workshops, publications; specializing in new product acquisition and diversification information services.

Shelfpower
Groat House, Groat Market
Newcastle upon Tyne NE1 1UQ
(0632) 24419
Key Individuals: S.E. Johnson, D.P. Sugarman
Industrial library design, library management, bibliographic searches (engineering and manufacturing fields).

Solon Consultants
23 Bedford Row
London WC2
(01) 242 2261
Key Individual: John Myers

Desk and market research, consultancy for business strategy and corporate planning.

Times Marketing and Business Information Service
New Printing House Square
Grays Inn Rd.
London WC2
(01) 837 1234
Key Individual: Christine Hull
Desk and market research, press cuttings, publications.

Transociates
139 Chevening Rd.
London NW6 6DZ
(01) 730 0855, days
(01) 969 2862, evenings
Key Individual: Thomas Landau
Technical translations, collection of trade literature; specializing in scientific and technological areas.

Warwick Statistics Service
University of Warwick Library
Coventry CV4 7AL
(0203) 62530
Key Individual: David Mort
Enquiry, research and analyses, alerting service, statistical and marketing information, on-line searching, document retrieval, bibliographies, publications; one of the largest statistics collections in the U.K.

Jeremy Weston
"Tarbert," 44 Stratford Rd.
Watford, Herts.
(0923) 29081
Research and consultancy for scientific and technical publishers.

SELECTED BIBLIOGRAPHY

MAJOR WORKS—MONOGRAPHS

Birks, Christine I. *Information Services in the Market Place.* Research & Development Reports, no. 5430. London: The British Library, July 1978. This is the only major study of "on-demand information services" undertaken in the United Kingdom. It is based on survey statistics as well as personal interviews with 40 services, most of which are research associations rather than independent information services. Includes a comprehensive bibliography of both British and U.S. works.

Duke, Judith S. *The Business Information Markets, 1979–84.* White Plains, N.Y.: Knowledge Industry Publications, 1979. An updated version of 1975 Goldstein report below; analyzes major segments of the business information industry—a $3 billion/year business. More than 20 firms are profiled with regard to key personnel, up-to-date financial data, and analysis of company products. Projections for industry growth are given.

Garvin, Andrew P. and Bermont, Hubert. *How to Win with Information or Lose Without It.* Washington, D.C.: Bermont Books, 1980, 171 pp. An excellent how-to manual with a basic premise of raising the reader's information consciousness. Topics discussed in detail include information-gathering techniques, computer databases, and information retrieval services. Written with the business professional in mind; a useful compendium of sources in the appendix. Coauthored by the founder of FIND.

Goldstein, Seth. *The Business Information Markets, 1976–81.* White Plains, N.Y.: Knowledge Industry Publications, 1975. The predecessor of the 1979 report above. Affords invaluable insights into the business information industry with regard to future trends.

Information Industry Association. *Information Sources.* Washington, D.C.: IIA, (Annual). Lists members of the Information Industry Association using their own descriptions and logos. Also used as an acquisition/merger sourcebook or guide by companies in the information industry.

Information Market Place 1978–79. New York: R. R. Bowker and Learned Information, 1978. An International directory of information products and services. Sold in Europe as *Information Trade Directory.*

Information Industry Market Place 1981. New York: R. R. Bowker and Learned Information, 1980.

Library Association of the City University of New York, Bibliography Committee. *The Information Industry and the Library—Competition or Cooperation?* New York: LACUNY, 1979. A bibliography on the theme of the LACUNY '79 institute of the same title, April 16, 1979. Over 100 journal and book citations under the headings "Fees for Library Service," "Information Industry Association," and "Information Services."

McLaughlin, Brian. *Marketing of Professional Services: A Bibliography, 1970–78.* Syracuse, N.Y.: Information Services and Research, 1978. (Information Technology Bibliography Series). A useful bibliography compiled by an independent information broker in Syracuse. (See directory listing for Information Services and Research in Appendix 3.)

Minor, Barbara B., ed. *Proceedings of the Information Broker/Free Lance Librarian—New Careers—New Library Services Workshop.* Syracuse, N.Y.: Syracuse University School of Information Studies, August 1976. Participants in this workshop were Susan Klement of Information Resources (Toronto), Carol Vantine of Inform (Minneapolis Public Library), Christopher Samuels of Information for Business (New York), and Maxine Davis of Information Access (Syracuse), each giving a short presentation and fielding questions. Appendices include sample discussion questions, sample contracts and invoices, directory of information brokers, comprehensive bibliography, and a checklist, "Things to Know—Places to Go—to Assist in Running a Small Business." Good introduction to the concept of information as an economic commodity and alternative careers for librarians.

Raffin, Margaret, ed. *The Marketing of Information Services,* proceedings seminar, Aslib Information Industry Group, May 11, 1977. London: Aslib 1978. Discussions on marketing of information services, user needs, pricing sales methods, advertising, and promotion; debated by representatives from commercial and nonprofit organizations.

Sellen, Betty-Carol, ed. *What Else You Can Do With a Library Degree.* Syracuse, N.Y.: Gaylord Professional Publications in association with Neal-Schuman Publishers, 1980. Based on a survey questionnaire sent to alternative or nontraditional librarians during 1978. Includes over 50 vignettes in 4 parts: On Their Own; Information Management, Indexing and Research; The Book Industry; Communications, The Arts, Education and Government. Includes the outline for Susan Klement's (Information Resources, Toronto, Canada) course, "Alternatives in Librarianship," offered at the University of Toronto and Kent State library schools. Articles by principals of fee-based information services—Alice Warner (Warner-Eddison Associates, Cambridge, MA), Darlene Waterstreet (Badger Infosearch, Milwaukee, WI), Norma Levy (Fact Finders, Ridgewood, NJ), Judith Mahrer (Library Services, Denver, CO), Judith Helburn (Library Management and Services, Austin, TX).

Warnken, Kelly. *The Directory of Fee-Based Information Services.* Woodstock, N.Y.: Information Alternative, (Annual). First edition was published in 1976; the second in 1978; the third edition in 1980, and a fourth will be published in 1981. Supplements for the directory may be issued quarterly instead of being published in the bimonthly *Journal of Fee-Based Information Services.*

White, Martin S. *Profit From Information—How to Manage an Information Consultancy.* Andre Deutsch, 1981 (in press). The author establishes guidelines for starting fee-based information services or "information consultancies" based on his own experience as director of a European information consultancy. Provides a checklist for marketing professional information services aimed at U.S. and European markets.

West, Celeste and Katz, Elizabeth. *Revolting Librarians.* San Francisco: Booklegger Press, 1972. Alternative libraries grassroots movement at its peak; several articles contributed by free-lance librarians and now famous information professionals. Good historical perspective to alternative library movement. Although now out of print, a sequel is pending.

MAJOR WORKS—PERIODICALS AND YEARBOOKS

Bellardo, T., and Waldhart, T. J. "Marketing Products and Services in Academic Libraries." *Libri* 27 (September 1977): 181–194.

Boss, Richard W. "The Library as Information Broker," Association of College and Research Libraries, 1st natl. conf., November 1978. College and Research Libraries, Vol. 40 (March 1979): 136–140.

Chanaud, Jo, and Chanaud, Robert. "The Independent Information Specialist and the Research Library." *Journal of the Society of Research Administrators* 6 (Winter 1975): 26–31.

Cuadra, Carlos. "Information Industry." In *ALA Yearbook 1977*. Chicago: American Library Association, 1977, pp. 160–163.

Davis, Maxine W. "A Quick Guide to Free Lance Librarianship." [bibliography] *Wilson Library Bulletin* 49 (February 1975): 445.

Dodd, James B. "Information Brokers." *Special Libraries* 67 (May/June 1976): 243–250.

Doebler, Paul. "Paul Zurkowski, the Head of the Information Industry." *Publishers Weekly* 203 (June 25, 1973): 38–39.

———. "10 Years Old, Information Industry Association Grapples with Far-Reaching Issues." *Publishers Weekly* 212 (November 7, 1977): 25–26.

Elias, Art. "Marketing on Online Bibliographic Services." *Online Review* 3 (1979): 107–117.

Felicetti, Barbara Whyte. "Information for Fee and Information for Free: The Information Broker and the Public Librarian." *Public Library Quarterly* 1 (Spring 1979): 9–20.

Ferguson, Douglas. "Marketing Online Services in the University." *Online* 1 (July 1977): 15–23.

Feverstein, Edward D. and Mishkoff, Adina. "FIND/SVP: An Idea Whose Time Has Come." Presented at Special Libraries Assoc., Denver, June 6–10, 1976.

Finnigan, Georgia. "Nontraditional Information Service." *Special Libraries* 67 (February 1976): 102–103.

Finnegan Mulligan [sic], Georgia. "Free Lancing." *Booklegger* 1 (1974): 42–43.

Fowler, Elizabeth M. "Careers—A Changing Field for Librarians." *New York Times*, February 7, 1979, D15.

Garfield, Eugene. "Future of the Information Industry." *Current Contents*, January 30, 1978, pp. 8–11.

Garvin, Andrew P. "Welcome to the Information Revolution." *Planning Review* (March 1979), pp. 32–35.

Gluckman, Paul. "Educating the Information Manager." *Information Manager* 1 (August 1978): 30–31.

Harmon, Glynn. "The Invisible Manpower Market for Information Scientists." In Proceedings of the 38th Annual Meeting of the American Society for Information Science. Washington, D.C.: ASIS, 1975, p. 79.

"Industrial Marketing: Selling Knowledge on a Hot Growth Field," *Business Week,* January 22, 1979, pp. 34 E–H.

"The Information Brokers: Can They Succeed?" *Bulletin of the American Society for Information Science* 2 (February 1976):
—Gaffner, Haines B. "The Demand for Information-on-Demand," pp. 39–40.
—Goldstein, Seth. "Information-on-Demand: A Brief Summary," p. 10.
—"Information Brokers: Who, What, Why, How," pp. 11–20.
—Lunin, Lois F. "Answer is Yes: Information Brokers Can Succeed," p. 3.

"Information Industry, More Significant Than Ever." *Publishers Weekly* 201 (May 1972): 28–31.

Kaplan, A.R. "Managing Resources: Information as a Corporate Resource." *Electronic Business* 6 (April 1980).

Kingman, Nancy M. "The Special Librarian/Fee-Based Interface or There's No Such Thing as a Free Lunch." Special Libraries Association, Contributed Papers Session, 66th Annual Conference, Chicago, June 8–12, 1975. Available on microfiche from SLA, Illinois Chapter.

————, and Vantine, Carol. "Commentary on the Special Librarian/Fee-Based Service Interface." *Special Libraries* 68 (September 1977): 320–322.

Kotler, Philip. "Strategies for Introducing Marketing into Non-Profit Organizations." *Journal of Marketing* 43 (January 1979): 37–44.

Landau, Robert M. "Information Resources Management." *Information Manager* 1 (August 1978): 10–12.

Line, Maurice B. "Information Services in University Libraries." *Journal of Librarianship* 1 (October 1968): 211–214.

Mauerhoff, Georg. "An Information Industry for Canada." *The Business Quarterly* 42 (Summer 1977) : 35–41.

Mick, Colin K. "Cost Analysis of Information Systems and Services." In *Annual Review of Information Science and Technology,* vol. 14. Washington, D.C.: American Society for Information Science, 1979, pp. 37–64.

Miller, William H. "Taming the Information Monster." *Industry Week* (January 7, 1980).

Monsen, Gordon. "Coping with the Demand." *American Libraries* 6 (February 1976): 72.

Nyren, Karl. "Information Entrepreneurs Stake Claims at LACUNY." *Library Journal* 104 (June 1, 1979): 1199–1201.

Payne, A. R., and Cleaver, S. "Information for Industry: The Research Associations' Role." *Aslib Proceedings* 28 (February 1976): 84–95.

Scarfe, David. "The Future Pattern of Information Services for Industry and Commerce." *Aslib Proceedings* 27 (March 1975): 80–89.

Smith, Patricia K. "Marketing Online Services." Part I, *Online* 4 (January 1980): 60–62. Part II, *Online* 4 (April 1980): 68–69.

Stern, L. W., et al. "Promotion of Information Services: An Evaluation of Alternative Approaches." *Journal of the American Society for Information Science* 24 (May 1973): 171–179.

Taylor, Robert S. "Information Studies at Syracuse." *Bulletin of the American Society for Information Science* 1 (August/September 1974): 16.

Valdez, Maureen. "An Information Broker as a Member of a Health Service Planning Unit." *Aslib Proceedings* 26 (December 1974): 473–476.

Warner, Alice Sizer. "Bridging the Information Flow: A View from the Private Sector." *Library Journal* 104 (September 15, 1979): 1791–1794.

————. "An Independent Librarian Looks at Information Services—New Use for an Old Product." *Wilson Library Bulletin* 49 (February 1975): 440–444.

White, Martin S. "Information for Industry—The Role of the Information Broker." *Aslib Proceedings* 32 (February 1980): 82–86.

Wilkin, Anne. "Some Comments on the Information Broker and the Technological Gatekeeper." *Aslib Proceedings* 26 (December 1974): 477–483.

Zurkowski, Paul. "Information and the Economy." *Library Journal* 104 (September 15, 1979): 1800–1807.

————. "Information Industry." In *ALA Yearbook 1978.* Chicago: American Library Association, 1978, pp. 149–153.

————. "Information Industry." In *ALA Yearbook 1979.* Chicago: American Library Association, 1979, pp. 131–135.

PROFILES OF FEE-BASED INFORMATION SERVICES (PRESS RELEASES, PERIODICALS, ETC.)

Aspnes, Greg. "INFORM: An Evaluation Study." *Minnesota Libraries* 24 (Autumn 1974): 171–185. (Inform, Minneapolis Public Library, Minn.)

"At Chase Manhattan Bank: Library Service for a Fee." *Library Journal* 103 (August 1978): 1456. (Chase Manhattan Bank/Information Center, N.Y.)

Callahan, Rose E. "Developing a World Trade Information System." *Special Libraries* 57 (December 1966): 575+. (World Trade Information Center, N.Y.)

Campbell, Tom. "Consulting Services for Business Libraries." *Edmonton Journal* (September 4, 1975). (Schick Information Systems, Edmonton)

Cheda, Sherrill. "The Free-Lance Alternative in Librarianship: An Interview with Susan Klement." *Canadian Library Journal* 30 (September/October 1973): 401–406. (Information Resources, Toronto)

Clausen, Mark. "What If . . . ? Computers Swift Aide to Information Firm." Cleveland *Plain Dealer* (July 17, 1979). (Information Specialists, Ohio)

"Companies Subscribe to Brokers' Research." *Business Week* (December 13, 1976): 67, 70. FIND/SVP, New York)

Cox, Clayton. "Ideas Can Succeed—Entrepreneurs Play Big Role in Information Industry." *Houston Post,* March 9, 1980. (Freelance Research Service, Tex.)

"The Data Base User: Chase Information Center." *The Information Manager* 1 (August 1978): 22–23. (Chase Manhattan Bank/Information Center, N.Y.)

"Document Delivery at Information Unlimited." *The Information Manager* 1 (December 1978): 27. (Information Unlimited, formerly of Berkeley, Calif.)

Doebler, Paul. "Seek and Ye Shall FIND." *Publishers Weekly* 202 (October 16, 1972): 39–42. (FIND/SVP, N.Y.)

Doerksen, Ray. "Public Forum." *Canadian Library Journal* 31 (August 1974): 345–7. (Commenting on Dean Tudor, Toronto)

"DuPont's Commercial Information Center: The Information Service User." *The Information Manager* 1 (August 1978): 26–27. (DuPont Information Center is an internal service.)

Fearon, Robert. "Found: One Answer to the Information Explosion." *Madison Avenue* 16 (March 1973): 12–14. (FIND/SVP, N.Y.)

Feinburg, Samuel. "From Where I Sit—'Information-on-Demand' Service Started with Student's Doodling." *Women's Wear Daily,* November 12, 1975. (FIND/SVP, N.Y.)

Ferguson, Patricia. "Chronicles of an Information Company." *On-Line Review* 1 (March 1977): 39–42. (Documentation Associates, Calif.)

"FIND: Information on Demand." *BCLA Reporter* 17 (January 1974): 19. (FIND/SVP, N.Y.)

"FIND: Information on Demand." Burroughs Clearing House 58 (October 1973): 30. (FIND/SVP, N.Y.)

Finnigan, Georgia, and Rugge, Sue. "Document Delivery and the Experience of Information Unlimited." *Online* 2 (January 1978): 62–69. (Information Unlimited, formerly of Berkeley, Calif.)

"Five Business Owners Share Their Company Stories," *Successful Business,* vol. 1 (Summer 1978), p. 5. (FIND/SVP, N.Y.)

Fragasso, Philip M. "Warner-Eddison Associates ?&!" *Bay State Librarian* 67 (February 1978): 7–10. (Warner-Eddison Asssociates, Mass.)

Fried, Dorothy. "Need an Answer? They Dig It Out." *North Shore Community News,* October 5, 1978. (Marshe InfoServices, N.Y.)

Goodfellow, Marjorie E. "Library Consulting: A View From Quebec." *Quebec Library Association Bulletin* 16 (April/June 1975): 3–6. (Independent consultant; no longer in business)

"Government Has Wealth of Data." *Purchasing* 84 (January 25, 1978). (Washington Researchers, D.C.)

"Have a Question? Try a Bureaucrat." *Journal of Commerce* (NY), August 24, 1978. (Washington Researchers, D.C.)

Holmes, Edith. "Company Profile: Warner-Eddison Builds Centralized Tools for Accessing Information." *Information World* 1 (February 1979): 13. (Warner-Eddison Associates, Mass.)

"Information Center Profile: Information for Business." *Information News and Sources* 1 (January 1975): 29–30. (Information For Business, N.Y./Mass.)

Journal of Fee-Based Information Services, Vol. 1, 1979. Available from Information Alternative, Box 657, Woodstock, NY 12498), $11/yr. institutions, $9/yr. individuals.
Profiles on Fee-Based Information Services:
"Profile: Info/Motion" (January/February 1979, pp. 5–6; INFO/MOTION, Lenox, MA).
"Profile: California Freelancer" (March/April 1979, pp. 1–6; Martha Ammidon Powers, Berkeley, CA).
"Profile: Facts for a Fee" (May/June 1979, pp. 4–6; Facts for a Fee, Cleveland Public Library).
"Profile: London Information Services" (July/August 1979, pp. 1–6; London Researchers).
"Profile: Taylor & Associates" (September/October 1979, pp. 4–6; Taylor and Associates, San Francisco).
"Profile: FIND" (November/December 1979, pp. 9–13; FIND/SVP, New York City).
"Profile: Washington Researchers" (January/February 1980, pp. 7–9; Washington Researchers, Washington, D.C.).
"Profile: Schick Information Systems Ltd" (March/April 1980, pp. 7–9; Schick Information Systems, Ltd., Edmonton, Alberta, Canada).

"Profile: LegWork Writers Research Service" (May/June 1980, pp. 7–9; Legwork Writers Research Service, Los Angeles).

Kernan, Michael. "The Facts Fanciers . . . From Cocoa Beans to Clothespins." *Washington Post*, March 20, 1979, p. B1, 11. (Washington Researchers, D.C.)

Kindall, Stephen. "Ask Uncle Sam." *Flightime* 11 (July 1979): 44–59. (Washington Researchers, Washington, D.C., FIND/SVP, N.Y., Information for Business, N.Y.)

———. "Knowing Where to Look." *Esquire,* October 1978, pp. 83–84. (Washington Researchers, D.C.)

Kleinfield, N. R. "Answering Questions Business Is Asking." *New York Times,* Business & Finance, October 6, 1977. (FIND/SVP, N.Y.)

"The Knowledge Detectives." *Modern Office Procedures,* February 1980, pp. 130–131. (Freelance Research Service, Tex.)

Krucoff, Carol. "FACTS: The Washington Goldmine." *Washington Post* (April 15, 1980), p. B5. (Washington Researchers, D.C.)

McDonnell, Lynda. "Research Done for a Fee—At the Library." *Minneapolis Tribune* (September 29, 1975). (Inform, Minneapolis Public Library, Minn.)

"Minneapolis Public Library Has Inaugurated a New Search and Deliver Service." *American Libraries* 1 (July 1970): 636. (Inform, Minneapolis Public Library, Minn.)

"Minnesota Library Group Offers $18.00 Per Hour Services." *Library Journal* 97 (February 15, 1972): 624. (Inform, Minneapolis Public Library, Minn.)

Mouat, Lucia. "Gold in Them Thar Bureaus." *Christian Science Monitor,* April 15, 1977. (Washington Researchers, D.C.)

"Newsmen: Source of Information for Executives." *Modern Business Reports* 4: (September 1976), pp. 7–8. (World Wide Information Services, N.Y.)

Omniquest Ends Search." *Millimeter Gazette,* January 1978. (Omniquest, N.Y.)

"Outside Legwork May Pay Off." *Inc.* 2 (January 1980): 26. (Arthur D. Little, Cambridge, Mass., Information Resource Consultants, St. Louis, Mo.)

"Packaged Facts Tells More Than Marketers Want to Know, Whether It's Blondes, Cigars, Irons, etc." *Marketing News* 9 (January 30, 1976) (Packaged Facts, N.Y.)

Persico, Joseph E. "Information—All You Ever Wanted To, etc." *Parade Magazine* (May 19, 1979): 19. (Washington Researchers, D.C.)

Robinson, Linda. "Washington Researcher Gives Guidelines for Getting Government Facts." *Houston Business Journal* 7 (March 6, 1978). (Washington Researchers, D.C.)

Saltz, Donald. "Tapping Stores of Information." *Washington Star,* June 16, 1977. (Washington Researchers, D.C.)

"Search and Deliver Service Designed to Serve the Business Community of Minneapolis." *Minnesota Libraries* 23 (Summer 1979): 53. (Inform, Minn.)

Shannon, Zella J. "Public Library Service to the Corporate Community." *Special Libraries* 65 (January 1974): 12–16. (Inform, Minn.)

Sherretta, Stephen B. "Singer Fingers Facts, Forecasts." *Tucson Daily Star* (May 4, 1980), p. D1. (Information Associates, Tucson, Ariz.)

Stevens, Mark. "Small Business: New Service Provides Important Research." *Newsday,* March 15, 1976. (Information for Business, N.Y.)

"The Supplier: FIND/SVP, A Leader among Information Brokers." *Information Manager* 1 (August 1978): 27. (FIND/SVP, N.Y.)

Trausch, Susan. "Their Credo: ?&!—Their Products: Facts." *Boston Globe,* June 9, 1975, p. 27. (Warner-Eddison Associates, Mass.)

"Unusual Business Venture Tried Here." *Westchester News,* Business Journal, May 18, 1977. (Omniquest, N.Y.)

White, Martin S. "Information Trader." *Library Review* (Winter 1978/79), pp. 206–8. (NPM Information Services, London)

"Women Mean Business: Librarians Form Research Information Service." *Long Island Business Review,* December 20, 1978. (Marshe InfoServices, N.Y.)

"Women-Owned Businesses." *The Executive Woman* 5 (April 1978): n.p. (Research Reports, N.Y.)

Note: Reprints of many of these articles are available through the information services specified after each citation.

REPORTS AND JOURNALS/BRITISH SERVICES

Birks, Christine I. *Information Services in the Market Place.* Research & Development Report, no. 5430. London: The British Library, July 1978.

White, Martin S. "The Designer and Information Broker." In *Information for Designers,* University of Southampton Fourth International Symposium 1979.

———. *Information Broking Services in the U.S.A.: A Report of a Study Trip, April/May, 1979.* London: The British Library, Research & Development Department.

———. "Information for Industry—the Role of the Information Broker." *Aslib Proceedings* 32 (February 1980): 82–86.

———. "Information Trader." *Library Review,* Winter 1978/1979, pp. 206–208.

———. *Profit from Information—How to Manage an Information Consultancy.* Andre Deutsch, 1981 (in press).

SPECIALIZED PRESS COVERAGE OF FIND

"Companies Subscribe to Brokers' Research." *Business Week* (December 13, 1976): 67, 70.

Doebler, Paul. "Seek and Ye Shall FIND." *Publishers Weekly* 202 (October 16, 1972): 39–42.

Feinberg, Samuel. "From Where I Sit—'Information-on-demand' Service Started with Student's Doodling." *Women's Wear Daily,* November 12, 1975.

Felicetti, Barbara Whyte. "Profile: Andrew Garvin, President FIND/ SVP." *Journal of Fee-Based Information Services* 1 (November/December 1979): 9–12.

"FIND: Information on Demand." *BCLA* (British Columbia Library Association) *Reporter* 17 (1974): 19.

"FIND: Information on Demand." *Burroughs Clearing House* 58 (October 1973): 30, 64, 66.

USER FEES/COSTS OF INFORMATION SERVICES—PERIODICALS

Allred, J. R. "Paying for Libraries." *Assistant Librarian* 63 (August 1970): 126.

Berry, John N. "Free Information and IIA." *Library Journal* 100 (May 1, 1975): 795.

———. "Comment." *Library Journal* 102 (February 15, 1977): 429.

———. "Double Taxation." *Library Journal* 101 (November 15, 1976): 2321.

———. "Fee Dilemma." *Library Journal* 102 (March 15, 1977): 651.

———. "Fighting Fees in California." *Library Journal* 103 (January 15, 1978): 119.

———. "Interlibrary Loan and the Network." *Library Journal* 103 (April 15, 1978): 795.

Blake, Fay M., and Perlmutter, Edith L. "Libraries in the Market Place: Information Emporium or People's University?" *Library Journal* 99 (January 15, 1974): 108–111.

——. "Comment." *Library Journal* 99 (March 1, 1974): 593–594.

——, and Perlmutter, Edith L. "Rush to User Fees: Alternative Proposals." *Library Journal* 102 (October 1, 1977): 2005–2008.

Blick, A. R. "Evaluating an In-House or Bought-In Service." *Aslib Proceedings* 29 (September 1977): 310–319.

——. "The Value of Measurement in Decision-Making in an Information Unit—A Cost Benefit Analysis." *Aslib Proceedings* 29 (May 1977): 189–196.

"Charges Condemned." *Assistant Librarian* 63 (December 1970): 192.

"Charging for Library Services: Must We—Should We?" *Texas Library Journal* 54 (Spring 1978): 46–47.

Cheshier, R. G. "Fees for Service in Medical Library Network." *Medical Library Association Bulletin* 60 (April 1972): 325–332.

Clark, C. "Charge for Service: The California Practice." *News Notes of California Libraries* 72 (1977): 17–20.

"Competition for Libraries and Industry?" *Information World* 1 (May 1979): 10.

Cook, J. "Financing a Library/Information Service By Operating a Cost Recovery System." *Aslib Proceedings* 24 (June 1972): 342–349.

Cooper, Michael D., and DeWath, Nancy A. "The Cost of Online Bibliographic Searching." Technical Report 003-75-01, sponsored by OSIS. Washington, D.C.: National Science Foundation, 1975.

——. "Effect of User Fees on the Cost of Online Searching in Libraries." *Journal of Library Automation* 10 (December 1977): 304–319.

"Cutting the Umbilical Cord." *Information World* 1 (May 1979): 10.

De Gennaro, Richard. "Pay Libraries and User Charges." *Library Journal* 100 (April 15, 1975): 363–367.

——. "Comment" by Annette Hirsch of Information Specialists, Cleveland, Ohio. *Library Journal* 100 (April 15, 1975): 702.

Dodd, James B. "Pay As You Go Plan for Satellite Industrial Libraries Using Academic Facilities." *Special Libraries* 65 (February 1974): 66–72.

Dougherty, Richard M. "User Fees." *Journal of Academic Librarianship* 3 (January 1978): 319.

——. "Comment" by R. D. Galloway. *Journal of Academic Librarianship* 4 (May 1978): 97+.

Ferguson, Douglas. "Charging for Information Service." In *On-Line Bibliographic Services—Where We Are, Where We're Going*. Chicago: American Library Association, RASD, 1977, pp. 60–66.

"Few Academic Libraries Charging Fees." *Library Journal* 102 (April 1, 1977): 752.

Freeman, J. E. and Katz, R. M. "Fees for Service." In *Annual Review of Information Science and Technology,* vol. 13. Washington, D.C.: American Society for Information Science, 1978, pp. 50–59.

Huston, Mary M. "Fee or Free: The Effect of Charging on Information Demand." *Library Journal* 104 (September 15, 1979): 1811–1814.

"Information as Fundamental as Energy." *Information World* 1 (May 1979): 16.

"Information Industry Promotes Libraries 'For Profit.' " *American Libraries* 4 (February 1973): 79–80.

———. "Comment" by Paul Zurkowski. *American Libraries* 4 (May 1973): 258.

"IIA Urges User Fees for Libraries in NCLIS Testimony." *American Libraries* 4 (June 1973): 335.

Kabi, A. "Use, Efficiency and Cost of External Information Services." *Aslib Proceedings* 24 (June 1972): 356–362.

Kertesz, Francois, and Cape, James D. "Current Trends in Making Information Centres Self-Supporting by Charging for the Service." In *First European Congress on Documentation Systems and Networks,* May 16–18, 1973. Luxembourg: Commission of the European Communities, 1974, pp. 245–269.

Kramer, Joseph. "How to Survive in Industry: Cost Justifying Library Services." *Special Libraries* 62 (November 1971): 487–489.

Kranich, Nancy. "Fees for Library Service: They Are Not Inevitable!" *Library Journal* 105 (May 1, 1980): 1048–1051.

Kreutzer, D. "User Fees: Libraries Simply Cannot Afford Them." *Kentucky Library Association Bulletin* 42 (Spring 1978): 16–17.

Lehman, L. J. and Wood, M. S. "Effect of Fees on an Information Service for Physicians." *Medical Library Association Bulletin* 66 (Janaury 1978): 58–61.

"Libraries for Profit?" *American Libraries* 4 (May 1973): 267.

"Library Use Fees." *Library Journal* 96 (September 15, 1971): 2722.

Linford, J. E. "To Charge or Not To Charge: A Rationale." *Library Journal* 102 (October 1, 1977): 2009–2010.

Lutz, Raymond P. "Costing Information Services." *Medical Library Association Bulletin* 59 (April 1971): 254–261.

Martin, M. D. "Pricing and Servicing Policies: A Supplier's Point of View." In *The Online Age: Plans and Needs for Online Information Retrieval,* Proceedings of the EUSIDIC Conference, Oslo, Decmeber 4–5, 1975, pp. 86–91.

Moisse, E. "Costing Information in an Independent Research Organization." *Information Scientist* 10 (June 1976): 57–68.

"NLM to Charge Fees for MEDLINE Service." *Library Journal* 98 (May 1973): 1422.

Penner, Rudolf J. "Practice of Charging Users for Information Services: A State of the Art Report." *Journal of the American Society for Information Science* 21 (January 1970): 67–74.

Plotnik, Art. "Issues Revisited: Free Services v. Fees-For-Services." *American Libraries* 9 (July 1978): 432.

"Public Libraries and the Information Industry." *Information Times* 1 (Summer 1975): 13.

"Public Library Inaugurates Fee Based Research." *Wilson Library Bulletin* 45 (September 1970): 98.

Robertson, S. E. and Datta, S. "Analysis of Online Searching Costs." *Information Scientist* 7 (March 1973): 9–13.

"Science Information Exchange: Charges Will be Made for Services Formerly Provided Free." *Library of Congress Information Bulletin* 27 (August 8, 1968): 475.

"Service to Business: The Fee Question." *Library Journal* 100 (June 15, 1975): 1182.

Shields, G. R. "Selling Out! Fees for Information Service." *New York Library Association Bulletin* 26 (January 1978): 1.

Skov, H. "Charging Policy." In *First European Congress on Documentation Systems and Networks*. Luxembourg: Commission of the European Communities, 1974, p. 339.

Slanker, B. O. "Public Libraries and the Information Industry." *Drexel Library Quarterly* 12 (January–April 1976): 139–148.

Stoakley, R. J. "Why Should Our Users Pay Twice?" *Library Association Record* 79 (April 1977): 170.

———. "Comment." *Library Association Record* 79 (June 1977): 326; (August 1977): 437.

Sturt, R. "Teaching Costing Techniques to Librarians and Information Scientists of the Future." *Aslib Proceedings* 24 (June 1972): 350–355.

Terry, M. W. "Voluntary Charges: Experience on the Middle Road." In *Information Roundup,* Proceedings of the 4th ASIS Mid-Year Meeting, Portland, Oregon, May 15–17, 1975. Washington, D.C.: American Society for Information Science, 1975, pp. 171–175.

"There Is No Free Lunch, But There Were Free Public Libraries." *New Jersey Libraries* 11 (April 1978): 4.

"To Charge or Not to Charge." *Library World* 72 (September 1970): 67.

"University Fees Spiral: New Charges for Computers." *Library Journal* 100 (November 15, 1975): 2094.

Urquhart, D. J. "Economic Analysis of Information Services." *Journal of Documentation* 32 (June 1976): 123–125.

Vickers, P. H. "A Cost Survey of Mechanized Information Systems." *Journal of Documentation* 29 (September 1973): 258–280.

Vickery, B. C. "Research by Aslib into Costing of Information Services." *Aslib Proceedings* 24 (June 1972): 337–341.

Watson, Peter G., ed. *Charging for Computer-Based Reference Services.* Chicago: American Library Association, RASD, 1977.

Wish, John R., and Wish, Mary Ann. "Marketing and Pricing of Online Services." In *Information Roundup,* Proceedings of the 4th ASIS Mid-Year Meeting, Portland, Oregon, May 15–17, 1975. Washington, D.C.: American Society for Information Science, 1975, pp. 143–158.

Zais, H. W. "Economic Modeling: An Aid to the Pricing of Information Services." *Journal of the American Society for Information Science* 28 (March 1977): 89–95.

SELECTED BIBLIOGRAPHY—MARKETING AND SMALL BUSINESS MANAGEMENT TEXTS

Aaker, David A. *Multivariate Analysis in Marketing,* 2d ed. Scientific Press, 1979.

—— and Day, George S. *Introduction to Market Research.* New York: Wiley, 1980.

Allen, Louis L. *Starting and Succeeding in Your Own Small Business.* New York: Grosset & Dunlap, 1968.

Baumback, Clifford M., and Lawyer, Kenneth. *How to Organize and Operate a Small Business,* 6th ed. Englewood Cliffs, N.J.: Prentice-Hall, 1979.

Becker, Benjamin M. *The Family Owned Business,* 2d ed. Chicago: Commerce Clearing House, 1978.

Brannen, William H. *Successful Marketing for Your Small Business.* Englewood Cliffs, N.J.: Prentice-Hall, 1978.

Breen, George E. *Do-It-Yourself Marketing Research.* New York: McGraw-Hill, 1977.

Broom, Halsey N. *Small Business Management,* 5th ed. Cincinnati: South-Western Publishing Company, 1979.

Cunliffe, Edward W., et al. *Fundamentals of Modern Marketing,* 3d ed. Englewood Cliffs, N.J.: Prentice-Hall, 1980.

Diamond, Jay, and Pintel, Gerald. *Principles of Marketing,* 2d ed. Englewood Cliffs, N.J.: Prentice-Hall, 1980.

Gaedeke, R.M. *Marketing in Private and Nonprofit Organizations: Perspectives and Illustrations.* Santa Monica, Calif.: Goodyear, 1977.

Hansen, James M. *Guide to Buying or Selling a Business.* Englewood Cliffs, N.J.: Prentice-Hall, 1975.

International Entrepreneurs' Association, Business Research Division. *SBA Financing: Existing Businesses.* Santa Monica, Calif.: IEA, 1978.

Jessup, Claudia, and Chipps, Genie. *The Woman's Guide to Starting a Business,* rev. ed. New York: Holt, Rinehart & Winston, 1979.

Jones, William M. *Survival: A Manual on Manipulating.* New York: AMACOM, 1978.

Kellogg, Mary Alice. *Fast Track: The Super Achievers and How to Make It to Early Success, Status, and Power.* New York: McGraw-Hill, 1978.

Kotler, Philip. *Marketing Management,* 4th ed. Englewood Cliffs, N.J.: Prentice-Hall, 1980.

————, and Cox, Keith. *Marketing Management and Strategy,* rev. ed. Englewood Cliffs, N.J.: Prentice-Hall, 1980.

Kuriloff, Arthur H. *How to Start Your Own Business . . . And Succeed.* New York: McGraw-Hill, 1978.

Lane, Marc J. *Legal Handbook for Small Business.* New York: AMACOM, 1977.

Lasser, J. K. *How to Run a Small Business.* New York: McGraw-Hill, 1974.

————. *How to Start Your Own Business.* New York: Cornerstone, 1980.

Leslie, Mary. *New Businesses Women Can Start and Successfully Operate: The Woman's Guide to Financial Independence.* New York: Farnsworth, 1977.

Mancuso, Joseph R. *How to Start, Finance and Manage Your Own Small Business.* Englewood Cliffs, N.J.: Prentice-Hall, 1978.

Mason, R., et al. *Marketing Practices and Principles.* New York: McGraw-Hill, 1980.

Mucciolo, Louis. *Small Business: Look Before You Leap; A Catalog of Sources of Information to Help You Start and Manage Your Own Small Business.* New York: MARLU, 1978.

National Society of Public Accountants. *Portfolio of Accounting Systems for Small and Medium-Sized Businesses,* rev. Englewood Cliffs, N.J.: Prentice-Hall, 1977.

INDEX